PEACE AND CONFLICT:
JOURNAL OF PEACE PSYCHOLOGY

Volume 11. Number 4   2005

SPECIAL ISSUE
Pioneers in Peace Psychology: Doris K. Miller

The Active Psychologist: Doris K. Miller   367
  Richard V. Wagner

Pioneers in Peace Psychology: Doris K. Miller   369
  Susan A. McKay, Mícheál D. Roe, and Michael G. Wessells

Being a Pioneer: How Many Ways and How Many Days?   387
  Ethel Tobach

My Colleague and Friend, Doris K. Miller   391
  Bernice Zahm

Doris K. Miller and Psychologists for Social Responsibility   393
  Anne Anderson

Peace Activism and Courage   397
  Milton Schwebel

•

SPECIAL ESSAY
The Risks and Payoffs of Skepticism   409
  Doris K. Miller

•

REVIEWS
Is There Really Hope for Peace?   419
  Marc Pilisuk

•

ACKNOWLEDGMENTS   426
INDEX   427

T0347928

The Active Psychologist: Doris K. Miller

Richard V. Wagner
Bates College

We are honored to present this Pioneers in Peace Psychology issue dedicated to the work of Doris K. Miller. As you will learn in the following articles, Doris has been a superior, persistent activist throughout her career—from her earliest years in college and graduate school, through her work as a professional psychologist, especially during her extensive efforts on behalf of Psychologists for Social Responsibility, and continuing today, mobilizing the forces for peace within shouting distance of her retirement community outside Philadelphia. The accounts of her never-ending promotion of the rights—and of the excellence—of women within American psychology are exemplary.

How active officers of APA divisions can be in political matters has always been a concern. APA has been reluctant to support or oppose—or permit division officers to openly support or oppose—some controversial social policy issues. As a result, the leadership of APA's Division (48) of Peace Psychology has had to be circumspect in its pronouncements. Fortunately, the Division's complement, Psychologists for Social Responsibility (PsySR), can and often does respond to peace and conflict issues with strength and clarity. It is not surprising, therefore, that Doris K. Miller, Activist, poured time and energy into PsySR.

In the ensuing pages you will learn from Doris' autobiographical interview conducted by Susan McKay, as well as from her colleagues' (Bernice Zahm, Ethel Tobach, and Anne Anderson) accounts, of Doris' devotion to the cause of peace and women's rights. Milton Schwebel uses Doris' career as an exemplar in his analysis of activism in psychology. In her own, concluding article—a previously unpublished speech—Doris eloquently describes a particular phase in her activist career: her attempts to "encourage" the APA to oppose violence in the form of the Vietnam War.

We are indeed pleased to provide this opportunity for readers to come to know Doris Miller, activiste distinguée and true "Pioneer in Peace Psychology."

Correspondence should be addressed to Richard Wagner, Department of Psychology, Bates College, Lewiston, ME 04240. E-mail: rwagner@bates.edu.

"We believe that lasting peace requires active political confrontation against socially unjust institutions and traditions .... The bylaws of the American Psychological Association state that the APA exists to promote human welfare .... (P)eace is a political process and (we) psychologists cannot abdicate the political dimension of our work."

*Daniel J. Christie, Richard V. Wagner,
and Deborah DuNann Winter,
Peace, Conflict, and Violence: Peace Psychology
for the 21st Century, Upper Saddle River, NJ:
Prentice-Hall, 2001, p. 386.*

Pioneers in Peace Psychology:
Doris K. Miller

Susan A. McKay
University of Wyoming

Mícheál D. Roe
Seattle Pacific University

Michael G. Wessells
Christian Children's Fund and
Columbia University Mailman School of Public Health

Doris Miller was born in 1922, the youngest of four children. Her parents emigrated from Russia in 1905, settling in Paterson, New Jersey, the silk manufacturing center of the United States. Her father, knowing nothing about the business, ventured into silk manufacturing. Doris characterized him as courageous and adventurous. Because his values encompassed concern about workers, he was instrumental in inviting the Industrial Workers of the World into Paterson to organize

Correspondence should be addressed to Susan A. McKay, Women's Studies, University of Wyoming, P. O. Box 4297, Larmie, WY 82071. E-mail:McKay@uwyo.edu textile workers. Doris' mother was an advocate for the underdog—a colorful and fascinating woman who quietly and personally helped needy families in many ways. She was determined that her two daughters have educations equivalent to those of her sons. Using her maiden name to avoid embarrassing her children, Doris' mother attended night school for adults and graduated with honors in biology and English grammar. Both parents were demanding of their children, all of whom graduated with honors from high school.

Doris entered Boston University where she majored in liberal arts, with a creative writing specialty. She became an editor of the medical school section of the university's newspaper. As a sophomore, she was one of the college paper's editors who unearthed financial malfeasance by University trustees who siphoned revenues from the bookstore. The trustees' actions were reported in an unauthorized edition of the school newspaper distributed to public news kiosks. Unlike the other editors, all upper class men who were summarily expelled, Doris was given the option of transferring without prejudice. Cognizant that she had no power to contest this decision because "I was an undergraduate, an underclassman, and a woman," she continued her education at the University of Wisconsin.

Her first direct experience with anti-Semitism occurred at Wisconsin when she was looking for student housing. Her maiden name, Koteen, signaled no special ethnicity, but when a potential landlady questioned her "origins," she identified herself as Jewish. "From New York?" she was asked. She was told that she could room only in housing designated for Jewish students. Certain that administrators in this famously liberal university would not tolerate this bigotry:

> I went to the Housing Department and raised hell about it. They knew about it and collaborated with it. I was very upset. This is what got me started in my Wisconsin activism. I joined the integrated housing movement led by a Black graduate student who was later arrested on a rigged "miscegenation violation." I was less concerned about the Jewish students—we had a variety of ways to secure good housing.

At Wisconsin Doris majored in psychology. From 1942 to 1944 she worked in Harry Harlow's laboratory, feeding and testing rhesus monkeys to record differences in their perception of form and color before and after lobotomy. These tasks from Harlow's point of view were the equivalent of floor sweeping, and the only functions permitted to female students. Doris and one other woman were the first and only women permitted into his laboratory for a 2- or 3-year period. Later, he apparently surrendered some of his misogyny—attributed by its victims to a past unsuccessful marriage to a psychologist. His imperious and intimidating manner accounted for Doris committing her only research "fraud": The monkeys' test behavior was so consistently reliable that any deviation was noteworthy. On only three random days of several hundred, their test behavior was agitated and their responses aberrant. On those occasions, she recorded but withheld the actual responses, submitting to Harlow test performance outcomes consistent with their predictable ones. In what Doris identifies as her first independent scientific inquiry, she reviewed everything she could recall that might have made these occasions different, finally realizing that the only common denominator, shown in her daybook, was her menses, so irregular that no *pattern* of aberrant responses had been established. Not wanting to hand Harlow another reason to discriminate against women, she mailed him the actual test results only after receiving her bachelor's degree in 1944, telling him in the cover letter her purpose for withholding the data.

While she was at the University of Wisconsin, Doris noted that psychology had little or nothing to do with the upheaval and protest occurring around issues of social justice: "There was no way in which I could integrate studying psychology with how I was living my life. It had no connection for me at the time." Besides, she planned to go to medical school and did not intend to continue studying psychology.

She was involved on campus with efforts to achieve integrated housing, and beyond those walls, with anxiety about the United States entering World War II:

> I hung around with groups of students who were deeply interested and disturbed with what was happening in Europe. I was not politically affiliated in any way. At that point, Hitler had marched beyond Poland. We knew something about Jews being exterminated, but we did not know that communists, gypsies, homosexuals, and other despised groups were sharing that fate. The newspapers were not reporting that as far as I can remember. That something was happening to the Jews was clear. That there was not a big hue and cry about it was clear. I was not a pacifist. I didn't think in terms of just and unjust wars. I knew there was something awful happening with this madman overrunning Europe and *something* had to be done. It wasn't until I got to graduate school that I became more politically informed and more impassioned about it.

During her senior year at Wisconsin, Doris married a soldier stationed on campus, who soon went overseas. When he returned in 1946 after their 2-year separation, they tried for a year to make the relationship work, but "We hadn't really known each other when we married ... we were too young."

This article draws on data from an interview with Susan McKay that took place in Washington, DC, on January 14, 1995. The interview traces her life-long involvement with social causes. Doris shows us how the early roots of her activism were fostered by strong family values. She is among the remarkable women of her generation who defied traditional gender roles to speak out passionately, engaged her sharp intellect, and demonstrated the courage to act upon her beliefs. This article illustrates the chronology of her commitment to act and speak out for social justice.

EARLY CAREER

Doris' first job for the summer following her bachelor's degree was suggested by Norman Cameron, her clinical psychology professor whom she described as "well-known and wise." Because he thought she was a gifted clinician, he recommended her for a summer job at a children's residential treatment center. She expected to be in charge of the girls' waterfront and doing "something else, too." When she found out that they wanted her to be a counselor in the craft and recreation department:

> I didn't know copper from silver, and in three minutes I made up a program for teaching current events and creative writing to be used for diagnostic purposes ... as an alternative to the recreation assignment. They loved it. The principal put together a classroom with 25 kids, 10- to 18-years-old, with IQs ranging from about 100 to 200. Boys and girls diagnosed from sociopath to schizophrenic. I was 21 years old when I was confronted with this. We were to meet daily for two hours in a classroom with no air-conditioning. It was an enormous challenge, but I learned an enormous amount from the kids. Other things I learned there shaped some of my future education and training.

She was most impressed with the social workers' skills in interviewing and relating to the children, and questioned the staff psychiatrists, psychologists, and social workers about their respective professional training. This miniresearch prompted her to apply to the Simmons School of Social Work in Boston where she was accepted for the following fall semester. The summer's work, therefore, moved her into an entirely unexpected career trajectory. She completed her coursework for her master's of science in psychiatric social work in 1946, getting her degree in 1947 upon completion of her thesis, "The social adjustments of the first 38 lobotomy patients at the Boston Psychopathic Hospital."

THE UNITED PUBLIC WORKERS' UNION: "THE MOST SEMINAL TRAINING OF MY LIFE"

After her graduation from Simmons and a year's work at a social agency in New York, Doris was employed at the Veterans Administration (VA) New York regional office, housing the largest mental hygiene clinic in the world. The size was important because many psychologists who had served in World War II were now interning at this office while they wrote their dissertations. Doris joined the United Public Workers union immediately and quickly became active. This union was considered

"red," as was any union militantly fighting racism. Union coworkers included not only professionals but semiliterates in menial jobs and bright people with limited education—groups with whom she had not previously experienced continuing relationships. She worked with them, ate with them, and went to church with them. The union was an authentic democracy,deeply formative for her beyond any other training she had.

> Very quickly, I became an officer. This was 1947, with Senator Joseph McCarthy riding high. It was eye opening—the most seminal training in my life, more important than my psychology training. I think that the trade union experience promoted the usefulness of my psychology training. It taught me a way of thinking that I could use in psychology. It taught me about what happens in periods of domestic political terror as the McCarthy days were. I felt that I was freer than any co-workers to do exactly what my conscience told me. I had no dependents to support. The men and women with whom I worked did. They were good people, but they were scared to death. Federal employees could be summarily dismissed more easily than private sector workers. For example, during Congressional Committee investigations, federal workers had the "right" to take the fifth amendment, but could be fired for doing so. So, many of my co-workers supported what the union stood for but were unable to put themselves in public-spokesman roles. That did not cause me to think less well of them; I understood the human circumstances.
>
> At one point, I had sympathetic psychiatrists contribute money "to keep their names off the union list." We needed money to defend the international head of the union who had been charged with contempt of Congress for not producing union membership lists.
>
> I was always very much involved in the fight against discrimination. Our union's number one concern was eliminating racism—especially outrageous in the post World War II VA. I have a photograph that I prize more than any other, leading a picket line in front of a VA installation. On picket lines, I always wore high-heels, gloves, and was meticulously dressed. I didn't fit anyone's stereotype of an anarchist. These were the first professionals to picket in a federal agency.

Psychologist Carmi Harari was also working at the VA at the time and carried a picket sign reading "Nothing is too good for the veteran, and that is exactly what he will get." Doris and others in the union were advising vets that their records at the VA were not confidential as promised and that these could be requested by the Federal Bureau of Investigation—for example, if a veteran applied for a post office job. The intent was to find out if the person might be a troublemaker for the federal government. Doris urged that people who sought help were entitled to security, advocating that therapists not record sensitive client information. She and her colleagues protested the release of client records that were to be used for this purpose.

Doris, as a union representative, testified in the U.S. Senate several times on the VA budget. Democratic Senator Joseph C. O'Mahoney, from Wyoming, headed the committee with oversight of the VA budget,

Doris K. Miller leading 1949 picket line.

Senator O'Mahoney was a very distinguished man. I think he had a background in the humanities. He wore a little string tie. spoke elegant English. He was the most literate member of Congress I have ever met, very courtly. He would say. "Ha. Miss Miller. you are a representative of the AFL or is it the CIO?" I said. "The CIO United Public Workers." The second time I came back. he recognized me [and] said. "Ha. Miss Miller. good to see you again. What do you have to tell us this time?" The next time we went down we had been kicked out of the CIO along with the Fur Workers Union. the Steel Workers Union [and others] that were expelled during the period of McCarthy. presumably as "red" unions. The Senator began to ask about union affiliation. I said. "Sir. you are so well-informed. I am sure you know that we are no longer part of the CIO. We are the independent United Public Workers Union." He asked. "Well. what was that about?" "May I set aside my prepared testimony and tell you?" I asked. He made the error of saying "Yes." "Our union has been trying to integrate unions in the South. One of our organizers was killed for that. Our veterans fought WWII to eliminate racism."

On another occasion, the head of the VA, General Grey, had ordered 5,000 health workers fired, although funds for these 5,000 had already been appropriated. Doris and her union colleagues worked to stop these cuts; she was spokeswoman. With the Senator's permission, Doris called on Alfred White, a Jamaican and VA Hospital attendant who worked with paraplegics. Possibly the first Black witness since Reconstruction to testify in the Senate, White said that he found it incomprehensible that although men to whom he gave care at the VA had been permanently injured during military service, their health care benefits could be reduced. Because of the hearing and the intercession of Senator O'Mahoney, 5,000 telegrams rescinding their dismissals were sent that night to health workers who had been given notice.

Doris also was involved in advocacy around the Loyalty Oath that was enacted in 1947 by President Harry Truman. This oath was required of any person entering the federal civil service. Federal union members understood that the oath was a weapon to squelch dissent by dismissing employees who challenged any management practice and was a precedent for other public and private employees. Other unions, rather than opposing it, saw it as a federal worker's problem and were embroiled in problems of their own. Doris viewed the Loyalty Oath as a whole new accusatory weapon: "At first the accused weren't told who the accuser was. Those targeted weren't even told the charges at first. Hearings were administrative, not judicial." Because lay people could represent the accused, a group of union lawyers were trained to help people in their union jurisdictions; these lawyers, in turn, chose some union members to train. Doris was one of those who was trained.

> I never lost a case although they were sent to Washington for reversals. The reason I think I did so well is that from the point of view of the administrators hearing us, being a communist was so heinous that it really had to be "proved." I don't know where they found the hearing authorities; they were sent out by Hollywood casting.

As a union activist, Doris was well regarded, liked, and trusted. She was among the few women holding leadership roles, and "they had a terrible time dealing with me because I was aggressive. My language was careless in terms of swearing. I cleaned that up. When I started, I wanted to be as free as the men were." After 5 years at the VA and with the union disintegration, she left the VA.

Because she was involved during vibrant years of union activity, Doris bemoans the death of much of the union movement. She views this outcome as a social and political tragedy that is related to the shallowness and increasing corruption in today's society. For Doris, the unions did a remarkable job giving people a feeling they could fight. "People who otherwise might feel hopeless had a sense of belonging, of opportunity, a feeling of hopefulness, a sense of being able to fight with other people against oppression."

Concurrent with her union activism, Doris was instrumental in the development of the Society Against Nuclear Explosions (SANE)—her first peace activism. At this time during the late 40s and early 50s, the federal government was pushing the construction of air-raid shelters. Public information on the deadly effects of radioactive fallout and strontium–90 and other nuclear residuals was being withheld from the public. Doris had a physician friend who knew geneticists and physicists who had testified as experts in executive sessions to U.S. House and Senate committees about the effects of radioactivity. The information, however, was not released to the public. This friend asked Doris to help disseminate information. To bring attention to the founding of SANE, they designed blue and white buttons because these were mental health colors and American Psychological Association (APA) colors. Because of the Attorney General's list of organizations regarded as "subversive," SANE was not a membership organization. It was an information bulletin subscribed to for $2 per year, to cover postage.

Within a few years, the mailings were going to over 10,000 people, exhausting their ability to handle the newsletters' distribution. Magazine editor Norman Cousins, who had brought a number of Japanese women burned by the Hiroshima and Nagasaki bombs to the United States for cosmetic surgery, offered to produce and distribute the newsletter through his office facilities.

Cousins wanted SANE to be a membership organization and arranged a weekend meeting for delegates credentialed by him to effect his plan; Doris was not issued an invitation as the New York delegate—she thinks because of her union activism. Undaunted, she attended the meeting through the intercession of a West Coast friend who transferred his delegate status to her. Using her married name (Doris Seldin) and armed with credentials, she participated in the meeting's discussion about organizing as a membership entity. Despite her concerns about the wisdom of becoming a membership group, SANE was organized in the mid-1950s, at which time the McCarthy era had been somewhat discredited.

Doris characterizes her activism during this time as social responsibility:

> Being responsible for what happens in the world you live in. Not necessarily being able to change it but not ignoring it or shutting out other people's views of what has to be. Trying to do what you can.
>
> Mainly, I view the essence of social responsibility as thinking—not withdrawing from what seems like such overwhelming problems that you say, "Gives me a headache; I don't want to think about it." Trying to think through what we do. Your orientation. Then your thinking becomes very important ... There are criteria that I think ought to go into one's orientation. I can't give a formula because it is inappropriate to say that you should be this kind of political person or that kind of political person or identify with X party or Y party. I think parties are not terribly distinguishable and when you think about social problems, you have to think about how they cut across class. How do they cut across gender? How do they cut across ethnicity? How do they cut across geo-political places where you happen to be?

Asked how peace and social responsibility interact, Doris responded,

> I have evolved what I now recognize as a strong economic deterministic view of history driven by profit and power. I wasn't even aware of this as it was happening … in a period of Bush's presidency where we chose to go to war, where we chose not to. I mean we haven't gone to Rwanda. I am not saying that we should. I am saying that we did go to Iraq in 1991 because we had oil interests there. Political-power interests are very clear and drive policy. The one criterion … is who pays and who profits? That can be applied to anything—legislation and policy. Who pays for this and who profits from it? It is almost never the same population, and that centers my thinking about an issue. They want to make more IBM missiles. Who pays? It is going to be taken out of school lunch programs. Arms manufacturers will profit; it's a way of sorting. It is the first rough cut for me. I think that peace and social responsibility intersect, which is the question which prompted this. The existence of peace and the non-existence of peace has to do with who is profiting, not who is being protected by the intervention.

GRADUATE SCHOOL, FAMILY, AND VIETNAM

The leadership in psychology in New York was made up of men who had served in World War II and were earning doctorates. The VA facilities were staffed by these veterans, who were given internships, and by area faculty members filling part-time positions. Thus, because of their activism, the thrust of licensing in psychology came through the VA. Doris was well known to these academic psychologists, who urged her to apply to New York University. So she returned to school in 1953 and ultimately completed her PhD in clinical psychology in 1964. From 1953 to 1955 she was consulting psychologist to the Walden School in New York City and started a psychotherapy practice.

In 1956 after knowing each other for 5 years, Doris and Joel Seldin married. Ahead of her times, she retained her Miller name "because my credentials were in it, and I wanted to protect my private life from any kind of intrusion." Doris adopted Joel's two sons because their mother could not take care of them, and she was therefore very involved in rearing them from an early age. At the time of their marriage, the children were 6 and 8 years old. With characteristic energy, she combined working, running a big household, going to school, and involved herself in the anti-Vietnam movement.

Her husband was a newspaper reporter and editor but not an activist. Lovingly, Joel teased Doris about her activism saying, "I am going to buy you a lamp post for your birthday, and you can lash yourself to it and protest." Doris characterized him as a superb father who, because he took a role in rearing the children, "freed me in a way that many women are not. This was immensely important and was absolutely supportive." It turned out that their very large apartment in New York was perfect for fundraising. One of Doris' hobbies is cooking, so she would "cook up a storm" for several hundred people. Their boys "would roll melon balls in ham and feel that they were part of the peace movement. It was marvelous."

Joel supported her activism by making signs for marches. Still, he questioned the effectiveness of marching, prompting Doris to respond, "Every time I march, next time one more person will march and more people will march. Each person that marches gives courage to someone else, and that's the key effect of it." During the Pentagon demonstration against the Vietnam War, the entire family marched.

There was a project that not too many people know about. Howard Gruber, who was a well-known cognitive psychologist and activist, and I started something called the Dolphin Center. This was during the early 70s when social action groups, which preceded the social responsibility groups, happened. Leo Szilard, a nuclear physicist, after working to develop the atom bomb actively sought to prevent its use. He wrote a wonderful book of short stories called *The Voice of the Dolphin*. The Center was a communal headquarters for social action specialty groups: teachers, physicists, computer experts, etc. Our objective—through common quarters, shared equipment and staff, and meeting schedules—was to reinforce each other's social/political activities and look at issues through the eyes of specialists markedly different from each other. This idealistic objective unraveled in six months, as groups other than our own failed to contribute rent and salaries.

Psychologists for Social Action was started during the San Francisco convention of the APA in 1968 while the Democratic Convention was going on in Chicago—the Democratic convention '68 at which all of the blood flowed. A group of psychologists whom I know were in San Francisco. I did not go that year. They got together to discuss the fact that the following year the APA Convention was scheduled in Chicago. They petitioned the APA to transfer that convention out of Chicago on the grounds that the activities there had been fascistic, and they did not want to meet there. It was the first such social political petition that had been submitted to the APA in decades. I have written a history about what happened much earlier. It was published in the *Journal of Social Issues* (Miller, 1972). It is very interesting because it covers things about the APA that very few people know about and should be reminded of every five years.

[The group] evolved and other groups organized around the same issue. It is interesting to me that certain social events occur, and simultaneously, [there is a] spontaneous emergence of activist groups across disciplines, across class lines. That was such a moment. All of the professional groups that had been planning to meet in Chicago for annual conventions immediately protested through their professional organizations. Even those who weren't going to be meeting there but were having conventions of their own felt absolutely obligated to comment on the brutality that occurred in Chicago.

Those psychologists who met in San Francisco were primarily New Yorkers with a history of activism from the thirties, forties and what not. They got together, and they invited others from New York who they knew would be interested. The decision was that this should not be a national organization as such. It should be autonomous, local groups because issues were different from locale to locale in a country as large as the United States. At a national level, we would be a group that was interested in the elimination of racism and sexism in the APA. We were organizing outside the APA to influence it in a way that ponderous governance procedures hampered within the APA. We wanted a policy that only equal opportunity employment observers exhibit at APA conventions. The APA had enough clout to require that. I am talking about a time when the printing budget was $1,000,000 in the APA. We said that was big enough to have clout with book publishers and that they should use that clout in constructive ways.

The group did many things. Rather uniquely, it agreed that when the group's goals were accomplished it would dissolve itself. [Subsequently] a women's committee, a Board of Social and Ethical Responsibility, and a board for Minority Affairs were established in APA, and APA literature was changed to eliminate sexism.

Black student psychologists were organizing at this time, followed by Black psychologists and Native American psychologists. These groups developed caucuses or organizations, and Psychologists for Social Action was instrumental as a "good broker" among these groups, important because competing factors existed which prevented them from working together.

> For example, we had a very prominent Native American male psychologist who certainly had very good values who could not support some of the positions of the Women's Caucus or the women's groups. His tribe would have been absolutely appalled by his acknowledgment of women, and because he was dedicated to trying to be a conduit between his tribe and the world at large, he could not be put in the compromising position of supporting women's groups. We brokered that so that the women wouldn't spit on him. We felt that not everything could be subsumed under a single need. One could not ignore the needs of others. If there was competition, you had to compromise in some way. That didn't mean that you had to compromise your values, but you go your way and don't condemn them for not participating.

All of these objectives were achieved in 5 or 6 years, and the group dissolved as promised.

Doris recalls with delight one particular highlight of this period: the first APA anti-Vietnam War protest march that she organized in 1970. The route went from

the APA building on 17th Street NW to the White House. She spent 2 weeks negotiating with the Washington DC police ("We're not the SDS [Students for a Democratic Society] but just a bunch of middle-aged psychologists"). She convinced
George Albee, President of the APA, to join her in leading about 50 other marchers
to deliver Ralph White's (1970) book *Nobody Wanted War: Misperception in Vietnam and Other Wars* to the Nixon White House. On a whim at the last minute, she
called I. F. Stone and asked him to meet them in Lafayette Park; he did, addressing
them and participating in a lively discussion of the Vietnam debacle.

THE EMERGENCE OF SOCIAL RESPONSIBILITY GROUPS

The second "eruption" of groups responding to issues of social morality occurred
in the 1980s when Psychologists for Social Responsibility, among other groups,
was founded. Social actions groups which had dispersed now reorganized as social
responsibility groups, with many of the same people involved.

> The only one that was organized much earlier was Physicians for Social Responsibil-
> ity, which has its origin in the voter registration period of '64 in the South. Young
> physicians volunteered to go down there to deal with the harm that was done to orga-
> nizers and people registering voters. They went as a medical corps that subsequently
> became Physicians for Social Responsibility. They were a domestic peace corps.
> There was an organization called SCRI—Scientists Committee on Radiation Infor-
> mation—comprised of what we used to call the Harvard, MIT, and Rockefeller Uni-
> versity axis. They were scientists, geneticists, physicians, and physicists. They were
> men who had been collecting information on the consequences of radioactive fallout,
> particularly in Japan. They were of totally different political persuasions, but they all
> had a horror of this stuff. They decided that the way to deal with this was to write a
> canned speech giving information. Nobody would vary from that speech because
> they didn't want it to become partisan in any way, but to become informative. They
> ... would go any place to speak at no charge.
>   I started going to listen because I knew some of the scientists who were talking. I
> think we were figuring at the time that something like seventy cents of every dollar
> was spent in military-related production. They were speaking in areas where there
> were airplane factories. I went to one such meeting one night, and I was appalled. I
> left with the speaker. I said, "You can't tell people they have to give up their jobs and
> have nothing ... . These guys moved out of the slums of Manhattan ... so that their
> kids could go to safe schools. If they can't pay their mortgages, they would rather be
> dead than red. You have got to have some alternative form of supporting your family.
> We need an economist. You need a psychologist to talk about anxiety in a nuclear
> age." I became their psychologist for a couple of meetings. I sweated that one be-
> cause we didn't know a lot.

Asked whether another important theme of her activism is the right of people to have information, Doris responded, "absolutely":

> We started in many of these groups with the assumption that if people are informed about what they are voting about, they can vote more rationally. It is to some extent a romantic ideal, but to some extent it is also authentic. We are not telling them how to vote, but these are the facts and these are the sources for the facts. We want you to know the sources are not tainted. Now, given these facts and given this issue about which to vote, what do you want to do about it? They may not want to do what you would like them to do, but that was really the background from which we were starting. We were trying to keep it non-political, but politically educational.

"GROWING" ACTIVISTS

To be a committed activist is not to act alone but to build an organization, including the mundane such as developing mailing lists, nurturing people, which means "holding people's hands, listening, and providing resources." Cognizant that far more interest groups exist today than 40 years ago, Doris sees today's activists as pulled in all directions and speculates whether enough activists exist to "mind so many stores."

Over the years, she has committed herself to mentoring future activists.

> Since I reached the age of roughly forty-five, I never accepted an elected or appointed position that was going to be of some duration without choosing somebody a half generation younger than me to train, so that there was someone all ready to take over. Once I hit sixty, I started looking for somebody a whole generation younger or more. I have always selected people who seem like very competent organizers among the young people ... to mentor and prepare them. I don't think people my age should continue in offices ... they should continue being active because their names mean something. They are trusted. They have got something to contribute. I think younger people must be brought into responsible positions, and that means elected or appointed offices.

ON THE ESTABLISHMENT OF AN APA PEACE DIVISION

Recalling how psychiatrist Robert Jay Lipton discussed psychic numbing and denial in a way that deeply engaged psychologists, Doris views psychologists as victims of similar numbing because of the failure within the APA and its divisions to deal with peace issues. She was opposed to a separate peace division (Division 48 of the APA, established in 1990) because she believed such a division would focus on research more than activism. Further, it would result in other APA divisions leaving the peace issues to one division. Instead, she believed that the issue of peace and war should be brought to every division to think about,

> How do you think war and peace relate to what you are doing? What is your obligation? Do you see your ability to conduct your teaching or your practice or your research in the same way in a world at war as in a world at peace? Do you think there is any connection between how you live your life and what is happening out there? I think ... people in these divisions would [then be] saying. "There are 38 major wars in the world. There is genocide going on all over the place. What does psychology have to contribute to understanding how this happens, why it happens, can it be stopped, can it be altered?" We say that we are the science and profession of human behavior and change. Why don't we test it?
>
> I think that people are in great denial and have great psychic numbing and as money dries up, their psychic numbing becomes even greater. They are competing for ... fewer and fewer resources. I think it is a very tough time. On a positive side, I think that the existence of a peace division certainly calls attention to the vitality of this issue. I think from an organizational point of view it is regrettable. *I think the existence of a peace division in APA doesn't let anybody forget that peace is a problem and an issue, but it absolutely exonerates them [other divisions] from doing anything.* (italics added)

Asked to reflect on the present and future challenges facing peace psychology, Doris views disarmament as a primary issue that must stay in the forefront. However, many other issues exist, such as exposing propaganda language used in the press and exposing government misinformation, as SCRI did on radiation effects in the 50s and 60s. She advocates for a voter registration campaign much like the one in 1964 in the South, accompanying minority people to the polls so they aren't left alone. Being an activist is a central part of being a peace psychologist.

Doris believes that a myth exists about minorities not being interested in peace and disarmament. When people are poor, unemployed, and do not speak English well, being an activist is difficult. Thus peace psychology must, importantly, be concerned about the economic organization of society, about creating sufficient job opportunities and reducing competitive violence:

> We need a new infrastructure in this country. We need new schools. We need new hospitals. We need lots of things that aren't profitable in the customary sense of profit. Peace groups have to be concerned with living-wage employment for human welfare. It is not a specialty of the economists ... not a specialty of trade unions. It is a specialty of people ... [something] that we should all be concerned about. Employment is a major issue because we are heading for structural unemployment on a permanent basis unless we reorganize the nature of our society. Technology has created surplus population ... we starve them, keep them ignorant, make them homeless, send them into a silly little war somewhere and get them knocked off ... government policies ignore the production and jobs required to provide a healthy and just society.

Throughout Doris' life of activism, she has held to her thinking about economic issues as absolutely basic and believes that more distributive justice for people is necessary. For Doris, "security means a job and bread and butter." She recognizes, however, that it is unrealistic to expect absolute distributive justice even though such conditions are necessary for real peace to exist. Real peace is more than the absence of war—it includes means to feed, shelter, and educate your children, and have access to all necessary health care.

STILL AN OUTSPOKEN ACTIVIST

With a look of inherent pleasure, Doris admits that she has been very outspoken and brassy throughout her life. She characterized her approach to activism as, "I just go smashing ahead."

> There is pleasure for me in not being afraid. The pleasure is not in being brassy. The pleasure is in not being afraid because there were many times when I have been afraid. I have been afraid of authority. I have been afraid of people in power who I know wielded it irrationally in a vicious way. I know I have been very visible. At the same time, I have been on every ethics committee that exists in psychology ... the "unfavorite psychologist" to many people who think I am too prissy about ethics, so the criticism comes from both sides. But it is wonderful not to be afraid.

Although highly skilled at handling controversy when she has chaired meetings, she can be very aggressive when she is acting on her own—aggressiveness that she controls when the situation requires.

Asked whether being a woman brought a different perspective to her activism, Doris responded,

> I was not terribly aware of being a woman [when] doing the things I was doing. I was aware of being a participant with other people; some of them were women—not as many as there were men. But I didn't have a clear-cut feminist identity at all ... . I think my husband was more of a feminist that I was, in a conscious way. I have had limited experience because I have been primarily in private practice since the real emergence of the contemporary feminist movement ... . I haven't had a lot of experience in the workplace. I hear some of these stories about women parroting men and their power, their exercise of power, and that scares me ... that offends me and hurts me. That may be a phase that must be gone through, until there is a shake down of another kind of exercise of power.

Doris continues to advocate for social justice in the retirement community where she now lives. As a pioneer in peace psychology, she has lived her values through her championing of social justice while bringing inspiration to those who know her. With residents in her community and like-minded nonresidents, she has participated in a weekly peace vigil for almost 3 years. Her seniors group has made common cause with activist college students for political discussions and lobbying on legislation of mutual concern, such as social security. Both students and seniors reject the President's transparent efforts to pit their interests against each other.

There is no day without a cause requiring attention.

BIOGRAPHICAL NOTE

Susan A. McKay, Ph.D., is Professor of Women's Studies and Adjunct Professor of Nursing and International Studies at the University of Wyoming. Her recent research has been on girls in fighting forces in Africa, women's peacebuilding, and Japanese–American women's internment at Heart Mountain, Wyoming. She is a past president of Division 48.

Mícheál D. Roe, Ph.D., is Professor of Psychology and Dean of the School of Psychology, Family and Community at Seattle Pacific University, and Visiting Research Fellow in Psychology at the University of Ulster in Northern Ireland. His ongoing research has two major foci—Pacific Northwest Native American modern communities and Irish Diasporan relationships to Northern Irish political violence. He serves on the editorial board of *Peace and Conflict* and recently completed his second year as Division 48's program cochair.

Michael G. Wessells, Ph.D., is Senior Child Protection Specialist for Christian Children's Fund and Professor of Psychology at Randolph–Macon College. He has served as president of numerous peace psychology organizations and is a core member of the Mellon Foundation Psychosocial Working Group on Refugees, which defines a global framework and research agenda on refugee assistance. His research on children and armed conflict examines displaced children, child soldiers, sexual and gender-based violence, psychosocial assistance in emergencies, and postconflict reconstruction for peace. In countries such as Angola, Sierra Leone, East Timor, Kosova, and Afghanistan, he helps to develop community-based, culturally grounded programs that link relief and development assistance to war-affected children, families, and communities.

REFERENCES

Miller, D. (1972). Social reform and organized psychology. *Journal of Social Issues. 28*(1), 217–231.

White, R. K. (1970). *Nobody wanted war: Misperception in Vietnam and other wars.* Garden City, NY: Doubleday.

APPENDIX
Brief Resume of Doris K. Miller

Selected Education

1944	BA Psychology (experimental/clinical), University of Wisconsin
1947	MS Psychiatric Casework, Simmons College, Boston
1965	PhD Psychology (clinical), New York University

Selected Work History

1946–1947	Psychiatric Caseworker, National Home for Jewish Children at Denver, New York Intake Office
1947–1952	Psychiatric Caseworker, Mental Hygiene Clinic, New York Regional Office, Veterans Administration
1953–1955	Consulting Psychologist, The Walden School, New York City
1965–1966	Professional Staff Officer, New York State Psychological Association
1986–1992	Consultant in Psychology, Metropolitan Life Insurance Company, New York City
1954–1997	Private Practice

Selected Elective Offices

1965–1984	Board of Directors; Council of Representatives, New York State Psychological Association President: 1974–1975 Representative to American Psychological Association Council: 1974–1976; 1981–1984
1974–1975	First Secretary/Treasurer, Association for the Advancement of Psychology
1978–1980	Chair, Operations Committee, Association for the Advancement of Psychology
1980–1981	Chair, Association for the Advancement of Psychology
1969–1972	Founding member and first Chair, New York Psychologists for Social Action
1982–1987	Founding member and co-Chair, New York Psychologists for Social Responsibility
1983–1986	Co-Chair, National Psychologists for Social Responsibility
1986–1987	Chair, Operations Committee, National Psychologists for Social Responsibility

Selected Committee Appointments

1963–1966,   Chair, Committee on Employment Conditions and Professional
1967–1969   Standards, New York State Psychological Association
1969–1981   Legal/Legislative Committee, New York State Psychological
             Association (Chair, 1977–1981)
1975–1977   Chair, Ethical Practices Committee, New York State Psychological
             Association
1982–2001   Board of Directors Standing Hearing Panel, American Psychological
             Association
1992–1998   Chair, Downstate Psychologists' Medical Record Access Review
             Committee, State of New York Department of Health
1992–1992   Consultant/Reviewer, The State Education Department, University
             of the State of New York, Office of Professional Discipline

Selected Honors

1960's   Several Meritorious Service Awards, New York State Psychological
         Association
1975   First Secretary/Treasurer and Founding Member Award, Association
         for the Advancement of Psychology
1980   First Allen V. Williams, Jr. Memorial Award
1981   Psychologist of the Year Award, New York Society of Clinical
         Psychology
1993   Karl F. Heiser Presidential Award, American Psychological
         Association
1995   Distinguished Contribution Award, Psychologists for Social
         Responsibility
2003   Lifetime Achievement Award, Society for the Study of Peace,
         Conflict, and Violence

Selected Publications

Miller. D. K. (1946). *A study of the social adjustment of the first 38 patients lobotomized at the Boston Psychopathic Hospital.* Unpublished master's thesis. Simmons College. Boston. MA.

Miller. D. K. (1964). *A study of differences between auditory and visual learners in respect to extraversion-introversion.* Unpublished doctoral dissertation. New York University.

Miller. D. K. (1972). Scientific societies & public responsibility. *Annals of the New York Academy of Sciences. 196,* 247-255.

Miller. D. K. (1972). Social reform and organized psychology. *Journal of Social Issues. 28*(1). 217-231.

Miller. D. K. (1986). Screening people in. not out: Comment on Morawski. *Journal of Social Issues. 42*(1). 127-131.

PEACE AND CONFLICT: JOURNAL OF PEACE PSYCHOLOGY, 11(4), 387–389

Being a Pioneer: How Many Ways and How Many Days?

Ethel Tobach

The City University of New York
American Museum of Natural History

Telling Doris Miller's pioneer story requires a book. She has been a pioneer all her life. She is an excellent critical thinker, has always been an innovative problem solver, and above all, her life has been guided by values of peace and justice leading to many ways and days of pioneering activity. The articles in this issue will give the details about her life activities. However, I want to share with the readers the most recent conversation I had with her. The result of that conversation is a good example of her pioneering ways and days. A good pioneer is followed by others who take up the goals of the exploration.

In "retirement" she is busy fighting for just and peaceful policies for the present national administration to adopt: out of Iraq; stop supporting the governments that oppress their people; use funds allotted to military activities for health, education, environmental programs, and so on. She does this by joining and leading the organizing efforts towards those goals by the people she lives with in suburban Philadelphia, and particularly with high school students.

In our most recent conversation, she asked if I had seen the latest issue of *Peace and Conflict* (Volume 11, No. 1) devoted to a dialogue between two military ethicists and various peace psychologists. She mentioned this because she was remembering an effort that we were both involved in during the Vietnam War. At that time, she had obtained a copy of the Psyop Counterinsurgency Manual (Headquarters, Department of the Army, 2004) dealing with Project Camelot in South America. She initiated a discussion with Division 19 about their activities as military psychologists. They were eager to talk about psychological remediation of the effects of stress on the soldiers at all command levels. They were loath to answer our questions or discuss this manual when we asked about the counterinsurgency manual of the U.S. Army.

Correspondence should be addressed to Ethel Tobach, American Museum of Natural History, Central Park West at 79th St., New York, NY 10024–5192. E-mail: tobach@amnh.org

This stimulated me to try to get the manual on the Internet to see if they were proposing the kind of activities that we had read about during the Vietnam War: how to get people into the village square and then to humiliate them in some way so that they were demoralized and less likely to be involved in dissent. I tried to get the manual by going to the Department of Defense for a copy. The Web site said "this publication is available at Army Knowledge Online, W.W./army.mil." What this Web site offered was Army Doctrine and Training Publications that are housed under "Series_Collection": The 20_Series_Collection lists FM-1-3-07.22, issued on 10/01/2004: Counterinsurgency Operations (Expires 01 October 06): The 33_Series_Collection lists FM 3—05.301, issued on 12/31/2003: Psychological operations tactics, techniques and procedures.

When I attempted to obtain these, I was denied access because of the following information on the Army Knowledge Online (AKO) home page: New User? Register for AKO; Eligibility: Active Army, Army Reserve, National Guard, DA Civilian, Retired Army, and Army Guests.

I then went to the Department of Defense online and was able to obtain the FM 1 3–07.22 Counterinsurgency Operations document, October 2004, Expires October 2006, Headquarters, Department of the Army document and print as much of it as I wished.

How does this show Dorie's pioneer leadership? She stimulated me to look into the issue of counterinsurgency. The dreadful news from Iraq is primarily about insurgency. This is a situation that the United States and its allies do not understand and that is causing casualties among the allies and the Iraqi people. It would seem worthy of discussion in any future dialogue between Division 19 and Division 48.

In the issue of *Peace and Conflict: Journal of Peace Psychology* to which I refer (Volume 11, No. 1), the only article that talks about counterinsurgency is written by Major Schrepel (2005, pp. 77–78) and deals with the French in Vietnam. On pages 86–87, the U.S. Army training program in moral dimensions of war and peace is discussed. In this article and in all the other papers, there is no reference to the Counterinsurgency Operations document that not only discusses Counterinsurgency but Psychological Operations and Military Police Support as well.

Events proceed at an alarming pace in Iraq, and it is understandable that this excellent issue of the *Journal* was conceived some time ago. I would like to suggest that the issue of Psyop's role in the counterinsurgency activities be the theme of another issue of the *Journal*, following some discussion by the two divisions.

Once again, Doris is a pioneer ... in many way and for many days.

BIOGRAPHICAL NOTE

Ethel Tobach, a comparative psychologist, has been active in various peace movements since adolescence. She worked with Doris Miller in the establishment of

Psychologists for Social Action and Psychologists for Social Responsibility. She has served in various elected positions in the American Psychological Association, including the presidency of the Division (48) of Peace Psychology.

REFERENCE

Headquarters, Department of the Army. (2004). *Psyop Counterinsurgency Manual.* Counterinsurgency Operations, FMI 3-07.22. Expires 10/2006.

Schrepel, W. (2005). *Paras* and centurions: Lessons learned from the Battle of Algiers. *Peace and Conflict: Journal of Peace Psychology, 11,* 71–89.

"I don't believe in peace psychology, I believe in peace activists who will bring whatever their expertise is to bear in the promotion of peace."
"Be sure you know what you have to know to use your profession in the most constructive way possible for peace."

Quotes from a telephone conversation between Doris Miller and Richard V. Wagner, May 16, 2005

PEACE AND CONFLICT: JOURNAL OF PEACE PSYCHOLOGY, *11*(4), 391–392

My Colleague and Friend, Doris K. Miller

Bernice Zahm
Sherman Oaks, California

Early in the 1980s, the Cold War was still raging. The nuclear arms race between the United States and the Soviet Union was in full swing. Everyone knew the extent of the nuclear arsenals that already existed, and they were still building and testing more, bigger, and better nuclear bombs that could destroy the entire world. It was madness. The effect was generally widespread fear and anxiety of a nuclear war between the United States and the Soviet Union. It was a time for conscientious people to take action.

Professionals within their professional organizations began to pull together to exert their influence, inform the public, release the closeted fear, and do what they could to stop the continuation of the arms race. Physicians for Social Responsibility were the first, I believe. They wanted to get the message out about what would be the human outcome if such a war were to take place. As psychologists, many of us also began to feel that we had a role to play. After all, fear and anxiety are subjects we are trained to deal with and the psychological situation was widespread.

I remember our first meeting. Alex Redmountain had arranged for us to get together at Carmi Harari's office in New York for the purpose of starting this new organization, which we named Psychologists for Social Responsibility. I flew in from Los Angeles, and it was there that I met Doris Miller for the first time.

I immediately recognized in Doris a remarkable person with a driving force, creative ideas, and a most likeable demeanor. She was fully committed to doing what she could to help bring the message of our newly formed organization to the public. We subsequently became close friends, and over the years planned and organized Psychologists for Social Responsibility meetings and programs together for the American Psychological Association conventions, as well as worked within our respective state organizations. Doris' ideas, commitment, and integrity were always an ongoing inspiration to me and to many others. As an example of the commitment she has made to Psychologists for Social Responsibility and its vi-

---

Correspondence should be addressed to Bernice Zahm, 4422 Sherman Oaks Circle, Sherman Oaks, CA 91403. E-mail: bsz@earthlink.net

sion, Doris has established a memorial in honor of her husband, Joel R. Seldin, wherein each year a journalist who best represents our vision is recognized.

I cherish the years we had in a close collaborative working relationship, and it pleases me to be able to honor and voice my affection for this dynamic woman, my friend, Doris Miller.

BIOGRAPHICAL NOTE

Bernice Zahm received her Ph.D. from the United States International University (San Diego) and worked for a number of years in the Los Angeles school system. From the 1950's to the mid-1970's she established and ran the Zahm School, one of the first alternative schools for children who "couldn't make it" in the traditional school system. Dr. Zahm was a key member of the original ad hoc committee that initiated Psychologists for Social Responsibility.

PEACE AND CONFLICT: JOURNAL OF PEACE PSYCHOLOGY. *11*(4), 393–396
Copyright © 2005, Lawrence Erlbaum Associates, Inc.

Doris K. Miller and Psychologists for Social Responsibility

Anne Anderson
Psychologists for Social Responsibility

"Good morning, Dr. Miller," I said, introducing myself as the new Coordinator for Psychologists for Social Responsibility (PsySR). Doris K. Miller, PhD, was one of the two cochairs of the Ad Hoc Steering Committee formed to provide a working representative body for PsySR as it developed its strategy for applying psychology to the problem of reducing the nuclear threat. Doris in New York, and Bernice Zahm in California, had agreed to cochair this distinguished group of colleagues that included Charles Ansell, Jerome Bruner, Albert Ellis, Jerome Frank, Eugene Gendlin, Carmi Harari, Ted Landsman, Arnold Lazarus, Rollo May, Sandra B. McPherson, Helen Mehr, Alan Nelson, Justin Newmark, Bruce Pemberton, Clara Rabinowitz, Alex R. Redmountain, Carl R. Rogers, Irma Lee Shepherd, M. Brewster Smith, and Nora Wexler, with Herbert Kelman and Ralph White serving as strategy consultants. And I, in Washington, DC, was starting as PsySR's first paid part-time coordinator, after Alex Redmountain, the founder of the national organization, had needed to reduce his involvement with PsySR for health reasons. So, on that day late in 1984, "Good morning, Dr. Miller," I said, and she replied, "What's this Dr. stuff? Please call me Doris." Whenever I think of what Doris Miller has contributed to PsySR, I come back to that first contact with her, which set the collaborative, teamwork tone that I think is a distinctive hallmark of how PsySR functions.

PsySR had been established as a nonprofit, 501(c)3 organization in 1982, based in Washington, DC, working out of Alex Redmountain's therapy office. Psychologists around the country who had also been organizing colleagues in their own locales quickly found each other and coalesced under the national nonprofit organization umbrella to work together at the national and international level. Today,

---

Correspondence should be addressed to Anne Anderson, Psychologists for Social Responsibility, 208 I St., N.E., Washington, D.C. 20002. E-mail:anderson@psysr.org

PsySR has members in almost every state of the United States, the District of Columbia, Puerto Rico, and in 40 other countries.

Back in 1982, Doris Miller had been one of those instrumental in organizing New York PsySR. Doris brought a wealth of experience in organizing and political activism to her post as cochair of the Ad Hoc Steering Committee of the national organization. Her work with Psychologists for Social Action, with labor organizing, and with the development of the Committee for a Sane Nuclear Policy (SANE; later to become SANE/Freeze) provided that historical perspective and depth of experience that the new organization and its coordinator needed. Together we developed the basic systems that PsySR required—membership years, renewal processes, elections, awards, and strategy for addressing the threat of nuclear holocaust.

Here's what she wrote in the fall of 1983:

> Psychologists have organized in the past to seek work programs during the Depression of the 1930's; against the rise of fascism in Germany; to eliminate racism and sexism in the (American Psychological Association) APA; against the Vietnam War, but the imperative has never been as potent as in the burgeoning development of Psychologists for Social Responsibility. Colleagues around the country are organizing to join forces with civic, religious and other occupation-defined anti-nuclear groups dedicated to preventing planetary murder and suicide. While other kinds of groups mobilize protests on political and moral grounds, the physical and behavioral scientists are assuming (as an article of faith rather than of evidence) that the human species in the large will act rationally to survive if provided with the facts rather than with propaganda. (personal communication, July 14, 2002)

She goes on to describe the acts of a psychologist and a psychiatrist who in 1953, "initiated a national newsletter containing congressional testimony on radioactive fallout" that contributed to the defeat of fallout shelter legislation, but "did not limit the proliferation of nuclear weapons." She also points out that Physicians for Social Responsibility and The Federation of American Scientists "have exposed as spurious the Administration assurances about the reliability of protection of defense against nuclear attack."

With this historical context established, Doris proceeds to describe PsySR's activities:

> Psychologists for Social Responsibility (PsySR) face a more complex mission less bound by "hard data," and formulate their programs consistent with local circumstances. Independent groups are already active in New York, California, Massachusetts, Colorado, Georgia and Florida and are emerging in other states; and a national networking PsySR is in the organizing process.
>
> In NYS [New York State] the overall mission is to utilize theory, research and practice to enable people to act in their own survival interests. A remarkable New

York City "how to" conference in February '83 has served as a model for other PsySR groups. Workshops were held on dealing with denial of anxiety, in small groups; assisting parents and teachers in responding to children's anxiety about nuclear threat; gathering data about reactions to danger of annihilation; working with community groups; learning about negotiating theory; establishing peace curricula in academic settings; working with the poor to relate arms-race policies to social-program cuts, and analyzing the distortion of meaning by propaganda on vocabulary.

She also set the tone of collaboration by noting that NYPsySR was working with several groups. This policy of working in coalition, collaborating with other organizations, and developing and contributing, where appropriate, psychological expertise to PsySR's sister organizations holds to this day. I can well remember discussing some particular issue on the phone and having her wonder what, for instance, the Center for Defense Information was saying about that. She was careful to be clear about psychology's purview and to ask for help from other experts when we needed that information. Her astute political analytical skills stood PsySR in good stead as we built a body of PsySR positions and strategies that focused on presenting psychologically informed information on nuclear issues.

We were not only educating the public, policymakers and fellow antinuclear activists—we were also engaging in ongoing efforts to promote greater social responsibility in the profession of psychology, especially as it related to preventing nuclear war. Doris also reported in 1983 about those activities:

At the recent APA convention, attended by approximately 6,500 registrants, the PsySR hospitality suite attracted about 1,500 psychologists during four days of conversations on nuclear issues: research reports on arming and disarming, children's reactions to nuclear threat, college students' perceptions of U.S./U.S.S.R. military policies, etc. PsySR co-sponsored six convention sessions in a "Peace Track" and became conspicuous as a growing activist focus. (personal communication, July 14, 2002)

All of this organizing with great effort behind the scenes, provided a venue for those psychologists interested in peace to find each other more easily. Eventually, the effort to launch a division of peace psychology was born. Doris was not in favor of the development of such a division. From her perspective we should have been insisting that *all* APA divisions take up the question of how their particular interests were related to building a more peaceful world. The Society for the Psychological Study of Social Issues for instance, had a long-standing committee on peace, which was disbanded shortly after Division 48 was established. We should have been insisting that APA as a professional organization become more socially responsible all the way along, and she has, over the years of serving on PsySR's Steering Committee and as a lifetime member of PsySR occasionally asked the cogent question, "What has PsySR been doing lately to press APA to act more in the public interest?"

Another enduring legacy Doris initiated, in honor of her husband, Joel R. Seldin, was the Joel R. Seldin Peace Award. The Seldin Award is an endowed prize for the print journalism work published each year that best addresses the issues of war and peace. The prize has been given for 15 years, and PsySR is now in the process of publishing a Joel R. Seldin Peace Award Collection of the winning articles. They include such luminaries as Molly Ivins, Robert Scheer, Noam Chomsky, and other less well-known writers whose careful and socially responsible work should receive wider acclaim. Doris has focused on how the media cover issues of peace and war ever since I have known her. She has understood the critical role media coverage plays in the development of exaggerated enemy images, and indeed, provided the leadership during her stint as cochair for the development of the resource manual on enemy image, "The Psychology of Enmity," which can be found on the PsySR Web site, www.psysr.org. That publication has just been updated, in response to the unfortunate enduring capacity of human beings to perceive the "Other" as a diabolical enemy.

Then there is the precious commodity that Doris has always been able to offer—wry, off-beat humor. She often would end one of our long, involved phone calls on some knotty problem with an off-hand comment—something that would lead me to think that she had just thought of another thorny topic to discuss with me. Then, she would launch into a story or a joke that would have us both hanging up the phone chuckling at the absurdity of the human condition. This was another valuable contribution to the PsySR culture: Always maintain a sense of humor in the face of overwhelming issues and insurmountable problems. It is health-preserving and so much more fun! Thank you, Doris Miller, for your wisdom, your persistence, and your dedication to the cause of peace with social justice.

BIOGRAPHICAL NOTE

Anne Anderson, LICSW, has been the coordinator of the Psychologists for Social Responsibility since 1984. She is also a clinial social worker in private practice with the Washington Therapy Guide in Washington, DC.

PEACE AND CONFLICT: JOURNAL OF PEACE PSYCHOLOGY, *11*(4), 397–408

Peace Activism and Courage

Milton Schwebel
Rutgers University

More than half a century ago, a psychologist's study revealed the need for peace activists to counteract public apathy toward the dangers of the atomic bomb. In this article, two types of activists are identified, conventional and unconventional. Both are motivated by the values they cherish, a sense of duty and responsibility, confidence their efforts will make a positive difference, and involvement with a community of like-minded people. Unconventional activists are disaffected with government, seeing no benefit in trying to change it from within. The roots of activism appear to be formed in childhood, the product of parental values and family life. The acquired values include a tendency to independent and critical thinking and the courage to make their views public, although these views contradict accepted government policy and practice. Doris Miller is presented as an exemplar of peace activists.

In 1946, when the United States was the only nation possessing the atomic bomb, Woodward (1948) studied a representative sample of American adults to assess their reaction to its existence and to inquire what they had done about it if they were concerned. She found that 50% of the sample was worried to a greater or lesser degree. Although most of the subjects referred to "the terrifying destructive power of the bomb" (p. 14), they had done nothing about it. Woodward attributed the apathy primarily to "a feeling of helplessness, a belief that there is little or nothing the individual can do about the problem " (p. 14). If people are not to take "a completely apathetic attitude toward the whole problem and resign themselves to Fate ... [they] must not only see the possibility of constructive action, but must also see what they as individuals can do to help solve the problems" (p. 14).

Woodward (1948) did not attribute the apathy and inaction to an unconscious defense mechanism like "psychic numbing," the validity of which was seriously

Correspondence should be addressed to Milton Schwebel, Graduate School of Applied & Professional Psychology, 152 Frelinghuysen Road, Piscataway, NJ 08854–8085. E-mail: mschwebe@rci.rutgers.edu questioned in a study by Locatelli and Holt (1986). She found the adults to be quite aware of the dangers, but unequipped to take action against those dangers.

This finding of more than half a century ago, in the infancy of the nuclear age, is not surprising considering that today individuals, and even peace organizations, are often frustrated over their inability to influence government policy and reduce the threat of catastrophic war. This condition exists even today when 87% of Americans favor abolition of nuclear weapons and, according to a poll by the Pew Center for People and the Press, a majority of Americans consider those weapons the worst invention of the 20th century (International Physicians for the Prevention of Nuclear War, 2005).

The implication of Woodward's (1948) study was clear: The American public needed information, leadership, and guidance if it was to combat the threats of atomic warfare. They could not get these from their own government, which was determined to maintain its atomic arsenal. It was determined also to maintain superiority over all other nations in the size and power of its arsenal, should any other nation, particularly the Soviet Union, succeed in developing the bomb. They could not get it from the mass media, which were cowed during the repressive era known as McCarthyism and later transformed into corporate global media that became in large measure the echo if not the voice of government (McChesney, 2001).

The needed information, leadership, and guidance had to come from the peace movement. Although the first peace organization in the world was founded in 1815, that organization and others came and went, and by the end of World War II, no active peace movement existed. People who favored peace had been embroiled for years in a brutal war and came out of it putting hope in the newly created United Nations. They did not anticipate the swift development of new and horrifying threats to peace and the long years of the Cold War. So new leaders had to emerge and new organizations had to be established—and all this in the darkening shadow of constraints on free speech and threats to the reputation, livelihood, if not the lives, of those who would publicly oppose government policy in the United States in the late 1940s and the 1950s. The new conditions called for peace activists to create peace organizations and a peace movement.

PEACE ACTIVISTS

A *peace movement* is composed of individuals and organizations that share a collective attitude that peace must be achieved through nonviolent means—preferably through cooperation, not competition, among nations. The movement seeks to shape public opinion so that it will oppose even its own government's policies if the leaders endorse violence in relations among nations, or between groups within nations.

Peace activists relate to the peace movement either as members of a peace organization or as individuals who share the collective propeace attitude and engage in antiwar activities as they choose. There are two types of peace activists, conventional and unconventional (Schwebel, 1993a). Conventional activists operate within the system. They seek to change its policies, perhaps by influencing the choice of candidates for political office, modifying the platforms of the major political parties, or promoting campaigns to alter government policy. Because they are within the system, they are more likely than unconventional peace activists to have access to the media, appearing on TV talk shows and op-ed pages in newspapers. Some are in strategic positions to influence the public, as in the case of Senator Wayne Morse, the first Congressperson to call for an end to the war in Vietnam.

Unconventional peace activists operate outside the system. They create and maintain peace organizations and seek to inform and influence the public through a variety of means including literature, the Internet, letters to editors, music, demonstrations, vigils, and picketing weapons sites. Unconventional activists differ from the conventional type in being disaffected with the established order or with the policies of a government in power, as studies in Germany and the United States have revealed (Kinder & Sears, 1985). They see little hope for change by working within the system.

MOTIVES FOR ACTIVISM

People become motivated activists, conventional or unconventional, for a variety of reasons (Schwebel, 1993b). They are motivated when they believe their cherished values, perhaps for peace, or social justice, or equality for races and sexes, are in jeopardy. Another motivating factor for both types of activists is their sense of duty and responsibility, maybe to their descendants, or to destitute people or victims of rape and other violence in war-ravaged areas. Political efficacy is a further motivator, that is, the conviction that their actions have a palpable effect on policy (Watanabe & Milburn, 1988). Peace activism, which usually means involvement with like-minded people, may be so central to their lives that they cannot forego their participation (Kinder & Sears, 1985). In brief, peace activism plays a significant role in their lives; as one activist put it, "in that sense it's given me an inner peace I've never had before" (Locatelli & Holt, 1986, p. 151).

The activist is driven by moral values. Elsewhere, in a study of moral creativity among artists, I examined the qualities that led artists to use their talent to address social problems, often at risk to themselves (Schwebel, 1993a). I asked: What led Beethoven to express his republican creed and his insistence on freedom and equality by first naming his *Eroica* (Symphony No. 3) the *Bonaparte Symphony*, when he believed Napoleon was a liberator of the downtrodden? What led Shaw to write a play about the business of prostitution on a large scale, *Mrs. Warren's Profession*, which was banned by the government's censor? What led Ibsen to write *A Doll's House*, which depicts a woman's quest for her own identity during the late

19th century, shocking Victorian-era patriarchal society? What led Picasso to paint *Guernica* after the fascists gave the world the first demonstration of saturation bombing to terrorize and kill civilians by destroying that city in Spain? What led to his determination to show the world what fascism unchecked had in store for humanity? What led Hemingway to reflect his strong antifascism ("fascism is a lie told by bullies"; Carlos Baker, 1972, p. 224) in *For Whom the Bell Tolls?* What led Lorraine Hansberry to write *Raisin in the Sun,* with its powerful story of how oppression of African Americans in the U. S. South can crush the spirit but can also be resisted?

Theoretically, answers to these questions are not very different from the motivating factors for social activism in general. Confronted with what they perceived as a malign condition that threatened their cherished values, these artists engaged in a transformative process. The evil condition aroused their emotions and ignited their imagination, leading then to their artistic response.

THE RISK ENTAILED IN ACTIVISM

Peace activism in general calls for courage, as I explain in the next section. Not all peace activists, however, engage in activities that put them at serious odds with their government and at risk of retribution and alienation. Many activists attending to poverty, hunger, and homelessness of the world's children, and of refugees in general, or those concerned about environmental degradation, do not arouse the animosity of their government—unless they publicly discredit government policy and embarrass a nation's leaders.

To find guidance in analyzing the risk prone activities of peace activists, it is useful to examine the work of an historian of science, Cohen (1985). In brief, he addressed the following question: Under what conditions do novel ideas arouse such severe controversy and conflict that the exponent of such ideas must have courage to put them forth? He was referring to novel ideas at the level of revolution, and he differentiated the scientific from the political–social revolutionary ideas. The latter, put into practice, might threaten the political and economic stability of the established order. "The scientific radical, on the other hand, threatens directly the current structure of knowledge or the status quo in science, but not usually in the society at large" (Cohen, 1985, p. 15). He went on to add, however, that forces outside the scientific community oppose some revolutionary scientific ideas, like those of Copernicus, Newton, Darwin, and Freud, because "they appear to threaten beliefs that are in some way fundamental to the social order" (p. 19).

With a few exceptions, scientific revolutionaries are handsomely rewarded with Nobel prizes and the like. Cohen (1985) contrasts the field of science with that of literature, where no equivalent rewards went to writers "of similar radical and revolutionary stature—August Strindberg, Henrik Ibsen, Marcel Proust, James Joyce, or Virginia Woolf" (p. 19). The relatively comfortable position of scientists, in other words, is not shared by those in other fields where novel ideas are perceived as a threat to the prevailing order. The critical point is conveyed in the last phrase, "a threat to the prevailing order."

COURAGE

It takes courage to take a public position that is perceived as a threat to the established order. Linus Pauling (Goertzel & Goertzel, 1995), already the recipient of the Nobel Prize in chemistry, took such a position before a subcommittee of the Committee on Un-American Activities of the House of Representatives, when he refused to reveal names of persons who had circulated petitions. He said the nation was in grave danger, but not from those who circulate petitions urging international law and international agreements. "It is from the stockpiles of nuclear weapons that exist in the world, which have the capability of destroying the world" (as cited in Goertzel & Goertzel, 1995, p. 180).

Pauling was a world famous scientist. Despite that status, not only McCarthyites inveighed against him; his own institution, California Institute of Technology, and some scientists were vehemently opposed to his outspokenness against government policy. When an academic superstar can be threatened with indictment and prison, it's no wonder that many faculty members in the social sciences in the 1950s were so intimidated that they self-censored course content (Lazarsfeld & Thielens, 1958).

Let us look at another scientist and activist, Albert Einstein. Starting with his student days and extending to his death, he was a fearless activist (Jerome, 2002; Simon, 2005). When World War I broke out, nearly 100 German scientists, including Max Planck, signed a manifesto supporting their nation's declaration on the grounds that Germany was protecting the White world against Russian hordes, Mongols, and Negroes. Einstein and 3 other scientists declared publicly that the behavior of the signatories of the manifesto was shameful. At least one of Einstein's three colleagues was jailed; because of his celebrity Einstein was not. That status, however, did not protect him after the Nazis came to power. Because of his continual criticism of German fascism, at home and abroad, the Nazis burned his books conspicuously and offered a bounty for his murder.

In the United States, Einstein's record of activism is equivalent to a history of struggle for peace and social justice from the 1930s until his death in 1955. Lynching, segregation, the West's blockade of republican Spain while Hitler and Mussolini were strangling it, McCarthyism, the abuse and mistreatment of Paul Robeson, the indictment of W. E. B. DuBois, the persecution of J. Robert Oppenheimer, unwillingness on the part of the United States and other Western nations to absorb Jewish refugees, the use of atomic bombs in Japan, the arms race, and the risk of universal death—these and other causes involved him actively and publicly. His participation in these struggles energized the peace and social justice movements, and earned him a bountiful Federal Bureau of Investigation (FBI) record (Jerome, 2002).

DEVELOPMENT OF COURAGE

Dictionaries define *courage* as a quality of mind that enables one to meet dangers with resolution (Webster's Collegiate Dictionary, 1947). Courage is essential in the first place during the intellectual process that leads thinking individuals to arrive at conclusions contrary to the status quo, contrary, that is, to conventional wisdom (Schwebel, 2001). In other words, before people become activists they must first transcend internal resistance to a changed perspective. In her study of creative people, John-Steiner (1985) found that they were not immune to internal and external inhibiting influences. Their strengths, however, were such that their new thinking emerged successfully in an inner battle against *the fear of exposure and the risk of alienation.*

Based particularly on his study of Darwin's notes, but also of the growth of creative ideas in children, Gruber (1973, 1974) explained that novel ideas develop very slowly, and that *individuals experience internal conflict about having a perspective different from the orthodox one.* In a later publication, Gruber (1986) identified characteristics of highly creative people, one of which is that such people are determined to hold to their divergent views and are able to withstand pressure to conform.

To become activists, after winning the internal battle, they must then possess the courage to share their novel ideas with their peers and the public. In other words, they must "go public" in criticizing government policy. What are the sources of that courage and what helps maintain it? John-Steiner (1985) found that the home atmosphere of her subjects supported their inclinations toward independence. Their parents valued openness to experience, and their teachers, mentors, and other models of independent thinking also influenced their development. When he was a child reading widely and extensively, Pauling had the benefit of supportive parents, and later, when he was under attack, he had the support of his wife, Albert Einstein, and other leading scientists (Goertzel & Goertzel, 1995). Peace psychologists, once their thinking leads them to take a stand, also enjoy the benefit of intellectual and psychological support from colleagues in peace organizations, as well as from organizations themselves.

To summarize, after Hiroshima the world required "new thinking," as Einstein put it. No single government was inclined to engage in such thinking, and the United Nations was too weak to influence the superpowers. The media acquiesced to the national policies and could not be relied on to provide the concerned people of the world with the knowledge and leadership that the times called for. Consequently, those needs required leadership and guidance from other sources, peace activists in particular. The courage of activists to break with conventional thought and to do so publicly appears to emerge from life conditions that foster independent and critical thinking. When activists take public positions that the established order perceives as a threat, they demonstrate a will strong enough to endure the risks of alienation, job loss, and other penalties.

DORIS MILLER, EXEMPLAR

Near the end of the now classic novel, *Grapes of Wrath* (Steinbeck, 1992), Tom Joad says goodbye to his stalwart mother, perhaps never to see her again. He had killed the brutal murderer of his friend whose crime was to try to organize exploited fruit pickers, and Tom was on the run, about to live the life of a fugitive. When his mother asks where he would be, Tom answers: "I'll be ever'where—wherever you look wherever they's a fight so working people can eat, I'll be there. Wherever they's a cop beatin' up a guy, I'll be there" (Steinbeck, 1992, p. 572).

Those words fit Doris Miller. Quintessential activist, she has been "ever'where." Whenever she has encountered racism, sexism, militarism, oppression, and exploitation, she has been there. Like Einstein and Pauling, and without the protective armor of celebrity status, she has exhibited courage in a life-long struggle for peace and social justice.

The biographical article in this issue (McKay, Roe, & Wessells, this issue) presents an expansive picture of her life as an activist. Here I will focus on those aspects that demanded courage.

From the outset, when she submitted an application for her first professional job—as a psychiatric social worker for the Veterans Administration (VA)—she was confronted with risk. Applicants were required to sign a disclaimer, that is, a loyalty oath, claiming they were not and had never been a member of an organization on "the Attorney General's list." This was a frightening moment. What organizations are on the long list? Furthermore, what constitutes membership? During the 1930s and 1940s, countless politically aware people signed petitions initiated by one or another organization to express support for or disfavor with government policy, just as they do now on the Internet. Was this going to be construed as membership? If I sign the disclaimer, Doris must have asked herself, what are the chances that I will be investigated by the FBI, or worse yet, called before the House Un-American Activities Committee? These fears were palpable and widespread among thinking people, and they set the tone of the time. Although Doris experienced those fears, she signed the disclaimer.

After making that difficult decision during those frightening times, one might have expected her to be cautious and "lay low." On the contrary, she immediately joined the union that had organized the VA and other government units—the

United Public Workers (UPW)—one of a group of unions that the Congress of Industrial Organizations (CIO) expelled for political reasons. During this period of terror (McCarthyism), the CIO deemed this group—"the red unions"—to be a liability. To Doris, however, the UPW was a source of strength and a safeguard for her and her coworkers. Furthermore, the UPW's positions regarding nuclear armament and war were consistent with her "cherished values."

The FBI was no stranger to Doris. Agents regularly came to her clinic, flashing their badges in the clerical pool and asking to see one union officer or another. These agents knew where to find the UPW officials; however, their aim was to intimidate the largely Black clerical workers and alienate them from the professionals who were their union representatives. If only one agent appeared, the purpose of the visit was to investigate a veteran on their rolls. If two appeared, their aim was to assess the "Americanism" of one or more members of the staff, Doris among them. She found this frightening but never felt overwhelmed.

Doris rose rapidly in the ranks of the union, to grievance committee chair and then chapter chair. These promotions in the union occurred for several reasons. First, she already was displaying qualities that became apparent in peace organizations some years later: inclusiveness and respect for all groups, verbal ability, leadership, and courage. Second, as Doris pointed out, men could not afford to risk dismissal (at this time men once again were the breadwinners in the family; World War II's Rosie the Riveter had been dismissed after the war and sent back home). Just as before, by accepting positions that made her a conspicuous activist, Doris voluntarily put herself in a vulnerable position. Public agencies had the authority to summarily dismiss employees for "disruptive" (read "union") activity. Although she had no family to support and could get by without a job for a time, she risked professional ostracism.

Consistent with UPW policy and her own values, she fought relentlessly against racial discrimination. In her first picketing experience she carried a placard reading, "Stop Discrimination in the Vets' Administration." This action was prompted by the VA practice of passing over Black social workers eligible for promotion in favor of a less qualified White social worker.

She picketed a second time to protest the FBI's invasion of veterans' privacy. In some cases, the veterans were applying for such "sensitive" federal jobs as mail sorter in the Post Office. In other cases, the veterans, usually Black, were considered to be "troublemakers." The picketing conveyed this message: "Veterans, we promised you confidentiality for your records. We can't protect them from FBI scrutiny."

The UPW joined protests against the Korean "police action," as that war was characterized. Members were warned to prepare for encounters with mounted police, to have in their possession nothing that could be construed as a weapon, not even a nail file, and to bring sugar cubes for the horses. During one demonstration, this urbanite who had never been close to a horse, found herself pressed against the wall of the historic Flat Iron building by a huge one. "I held out my hand with sugar cubes and the horse lapped them up. The cop laughed and pulled his horse away. I was shaken" (D. Miller, personal communication, April 10, 2005).

One of her heroes was her apartment house doorman. At this time in the 50's a Congressional Committee was investigating a number of unions suspected of being un-American and were demanding membership lists. One day the doorman told her that FBI agents had searched her apartment and also instructed him to save her trash. They threatened to punish him if he informed Doris. She knew the union offices had been searched, but this secret invasion of her privacy was frightening.

Doris was union treasurer at the time but was not one of the witnesses called before this Congressional Committee. Nevertheless, she played an important role: For 3 days, as she sat at the hearings, the membership list was "under my butt."

The union staff attorney instructed members about their rights and how to safeguard them in encounters with the FBI. When agents approached her in her office or apartment, she politely asked for their names and phone numbers and promised to inform them when her attorney was available to accompany her.

The superb quality of her professional work was somewhat of a protection within the VA. About 6 months after she started she was offered a promotion to supervisor, an opportunity she turned down because, as part of management, she would have been ineligible for union membership. Ironically, her bosses found her useful as "window dressing." Whenever union members complained about antiunion practices, management pointed to the "militant union rep" in their midst.

Besides her union involvement, in the early 1950s Doris served as one of the founders of what ultimately became SANE (Society Against Nuclear Explosions). First only a newsletter to avoid organizational status and the long hand of the Attorney General's list, it served nevertheless to inform the public of information withheld by the Federal Government, particularly testimony presented by geneticists, nuclear physicists, and other experts at Congressional Executive Sessions about the true dangers of radioactive fallout. Here, too, in her first involvement with a peace organization she and her colleagues had to tread carefully.

These frightening experiences during this period of terror in the United States prepared Doris for the struggles ahead, none of which she found as emotionally draining. During the next half century she participated, often in a leadership position, in struggles for civil rights, women's rights, against ethnocentrism, against the war in Vietnam, Reagan's blithe acceptance of the possibility of limited nuclear war (in Europe, of course), against the nuclear armament race, and the wars in the Persian Gulf and Iraq. When she retired and sought a stimulating environment where health care would be available, she chose a retirement community in Pennsylvania, halfway between New York and Washington, her two primary activity settings. This community, established primarily by Quaker faculty of Swarthmore and Haverford Colleges for their own retirement, offered her congenial neighbors. In typical Miller fashion, in no time she was involved with activist senior groups.

BECOMING A PEACE ACTIVIST

Doris has been a conventional and unconventional peace activist, the former, for example, as a member of APA seeking to move it in a peace-oriented direction, and the latter, as a leader and member of the UPW, SANE, New York State Psychologists for Social Action and Psychologists for Social Responsibility. In both roles, consistent with theory on activism, she has reacted to what she perceived as threats to her cherished values and has done so with confidence that her efforts would pay off. These organizations, in particular the people with whom she has worked, have been central to her life. So far as courage is concerned, she has exhibited that from her earliest days, in particular, when she initiated an elementary school newspaper and suffered temporary expulsion for an article she wrote (McKay, Roe, & Wessells, this issue). She exhibited it, too, in her UPW union years during the McCarthy period, and up to this very time in struggling against the Iraq War and other follies of the Bush–Cheney presidency.

According to the theory I presented earlier, the source springs of such activism and courage may be found in a person's early years. In the biographical article in this issue, McKay et al. (this issue) put it this way: "Doris shows us how the early roots of her activism were fostered by strong family values" (p. 371). Her father, of working class origins, was, in Doris' words, "courageous and adventurous." Although a businessman himself, his concern about the welfare of workers led him, nevertheless, to play a major role in bringing the International Workers of the World to his community to organize textile workers. Doris described her mother as "an advocate for the underdog ... a highly personal activist ... a consummate activist" (p. 370). Growing up in that setting where generally accepted viewpoints were challenged, it is hardly surprising that she became a popular lecturer on *The Risks and Payoffs of Skepticism* (Miller, 1986).

Combine those family values and parental activism with high parental expectations for academic achievement—and all this in an exuberant child—and you produce the "consummate activist" that Doris became. She became—she is—the answer to the implicit need that Patricia Woodward identified in 1948: leadership, guidance, and knowledge for the many Americans, and presumably people around the world, who are concerned about the state of the world but do not know what to do about it.

Most people do not have the opportunity to acquire the roots of activism in their childhood. Just as their parents before them, they are trained at home and in school to accept what they are taught and not to challenge their teachers or other authorities, as I pointed out elsewhere (Schwebel, 2003). Consequently, they are quite unprepared to question what they are fed by their government and the media. The difficult task of opening their eyes is left to the activist.

BIOGRAPHICAL NOTE

Milton Schwebel, Emeritus Professor of Psychology in the Graduate School of Applied and Professional Psychology at Rutgers University, was formerly Dean of its Graduate School of Education. His most recent book, *Remaking America's Three School Systems: Now Separate and Unequal*, was published by Scarecrow Press. He is a former President of Psychologists for Social Responsibility.

REFERENCES

Baker, C. (1972). *Hemingway: The writer as artist* (4th ed.). Princeton, NJ: Princeton University Press.
Cohen, I. B. (1985). *Revolution in science*. Cambridge, MA: Cambridge University Press.
Goertzel, T., & Goertzel, B. (1995). *Linus Pauling: A life in science and politics*. New York: Basic Books.
Gruber, H. E. (1973). Courage and cognitive growth in children and scientists. In M. Schwebel & J. Raph (Eds.), *Piaget in the classroom* (pp. 73–108). New York: Basic Books.
Gruber, H. E. (1974). *Darwin on man*. New York: Basic Books.
Gruber, H. E. (1986). Creative reactions to life under the nuclear sword. In M. Schwebel (Ed.), *Mental health implicatations of life in the nuclear age*, 314–326. White Plains: M. E. Sharpe.
International Physicians for the Prevention of Nuclear War. (2005). *Pew poll on the worst invention*. *IPPNW nuclear facts*. Retrieved May 18, 2005, from www.ippnw_student.org/nuclear facts.htr
Jerome, F. (2002). *The Einstein file: J. Edgar Hoover's secret war against the world's most famous scientist*. New York: St. Martin's Press/Griffin.
John-Steiner, V. (1985). *Notebooks of the mind: Explorations of thinking*. Albuquerque: University of New Mexico Press.
Kinder, D. R., & Sears, D. O. (1985). Public opinion and political action. In G. Lindsey & E. Aronson (Eds.), *Handbook of social psychology* (Vol. 2, 3rd ed., pp. 659–741). New York: Random House.
Lazarsfeld, P., & Thielens, W. (1958). *Academic mind: Social science in a time of crisis*. Glencoe, IL: Free Press.
Locatelli, M. G., & Holt, R. R. (1986). Antinuclear activism, psychic numbing, and mental health. *International Journal of Mental Health, 15*, 143–161.
McChesney, R. W. (2001). Global media, neoliberalism and imperialism. *Monthly Review, 52*(10), 1–19.
Miller, D. (1986). *The risks and payoffs of skepticism*. Lecture at Pace University. Unpublished manuscript.
Schwebel, M. (1993a). Moral creativity as artistic transformation. *Creativity Research Journal, 6*(1 & 2), 65–81.
Schwebel, M. (1993b). What moves the peace movement. In V. K. Kool (Ed.), *Nonviolence: Social and psychological issues* (pp. 59–78). Lanham, MD: University Press of America.
Schwebel, M. (2001). Creativity, conflict and courage. In S. Nagel (Ed.), *The handbook of policy creativity* (Vol. III, pp. 57–68). Huntington, NY: Nova Science Publishers.

Schwebel, M (2003). *Remaking America's three school systems: Now separate and unequal.* Lanham. MD: Scarecrow Press.

Simon, J. J. (2005). Albert Einstein, radical. *Monthly Review, 57*(1), 1–12.

Steinbeck, J. (1992). *Grapes of wrath.* New York: Penguin Books.

Watanabe, P. Y., & Milburn, M. A. (1988). Activism against Armageddon: Some predictions of nuclear-related political behavior. *Political Psychology, 9,* 459–470.

Webster's Collegiate Dictionary, 5th Edition. (1947). Springfield, MA: G & C Merriam Co.

Woodward, P. (1948). How do the American people feel about the atomic bomb? *Journal of Social Issues, 4*(1), 7–14.

PEACE AND CONFLICT: JOURNAL OF PEACE PSYCHOLOGY, *11*(4), 409–418

The Risks and Payoffs of Skepticism

Doris K. Miller

Haverford, Pennsylvania

PROLOGUE

During the Cold War my hard-nosed journalist spouse periodically declared, "Psychologists should collectively address, *exclusively*, the question 'Are humans capable of behaving rationally in the service of their own survival?'" My repeated flippant reply was always, "We don't have to study that. We know the answer is 'No.'"

Nonetheless, his question has ever since piqued and guided my scrutiny of mass behavior—particularly how mass irrational behavior evolves and, at its most lethal, accedes to elective war. Implicit is my assumption that war, other than in defense of aggression against one's own country or that of an ally, is manufactured by a powerful few and thrust upon the many. Motives of the powerful few vary: greed for more power or wealth, perverted religious fervor, fear of others' power, control of limited but essential resources.

Whatever the form of government, totalitarian or democratic, political leaders historically have tried to induce the masses to embrace—or, at least, accept—their rationalizations for promoting elective armed combat. The inducing and selling process is propaganda, widely regarded as inherently deceitful. If that were so, evaluating its merits would be easier than, in fact, it is.

The etymology of *propaganda*, as I surmised, derives from the same root as *propagate*. The term was first used in the Roman Curia, the administrative and judicial institution through which the pope governs the Church (*Encyclopedia Britannica*, 11th ed., Vol.7, p. 639). In 1627 Pope Urban VIII founded The College of Propaganda for educating missionaries to spread the news, i.e., the gospel (*Encyclopedia Britannica*, Vol. 27, p. 791). The Propaganda was religious and political, expressing a message and seeking believers. Today, propaganda still expresses a message, seeks believers, and promotes action.

If the message is not deliberately deceitful, or warped by its architect's defective vision, propaganda is morally neutral—just straight forward advertising.

Correspondence should be addressed to Doris K. Miller, 3300 Darby Road, #7201, Haverford, PA 19041–1074.

Until I recognized this elementary truth I thought we could teach people to identify deceptive propaganda; to resist its repetitive, seductive brainwashing, freeing them to act rationally in the service of their own survival. Alas, identifying deception requires knowing how to evaluate "facts" about unfamiliar subjects or events, feeling the right to exercise skepticism toward experts who urge that "thinking" should be left to them. How do we, in our culture, acquire information, which ultimately prepares us to evaluate authority, and challenge irrational or deceptive authority?

I was invited to address a January 1986 Pace University conference on "Peace and War, What You Can Do About Them." Based on faculty descriptions of the student body as substantially first-generation college enrollees from several ethnic backgrounds whose cultures and religions shared a heavy emphasis on compliance, I considered how to introduce the empowering idea that they could evaluate the written and spoken word of "authorities." Wishing to illustrate this possibility through an example unlikely to offend their values, I tried to find public school history textbooks about the U.S. Civil War written from Southerners' and Northerners' perspectives. In the New York City libraries I visited I could find *none* written from a Southern point of view. I did, however, find a volume about how textbooks were written, about which, more later.

My talk was titled "The Risks and Payoffs of Skepticism," and took place 3 days before the space shuttle, Challenger, exploded on launching. I have never submitted the talk for publication. Because I regard it to be as relevant today as it was 17½ years ago, and my mission continues to be the promotion of skeptical scrutiny of what we are told, especially by political powers, I submit this adapted version now in acknowledgment and appreciation of Division 48's 2003 Lifetime Achievement Award.

THE RISKS AND PAYOFFS OF SKEPTICISM

A volatile combination of circumstances accounts for my selection of this topic. The quantum leap in nuclear destructive power since the United States dropped the first atom bomb on Hiroshima on August 6, 1945, has wiped out any safety barrier between Them and Us. A weapon powerful enough to destroy Them will have a boomerang effect on Us. At the same time, technology for information management has undergone an equivalent quantum leap in sophistication. This convergence of technologies is good and sufficient cause for the exercise of skepticism.

The skepticism I advocate is not the formal philosophical kind but rather the vernacular variety: "Would you buy a used car from this man?" The question is usually a caption under an unappealing photograph, but for our purposes this example is a live situation. Now, consider the assumptions in the question. The shopper knows little about cars and therefore must rely on the salesman's knowledge and honesty. However, the shopper's technical ignorance precludes an informed judgment about the seller's knowledge, thus a judgment about his honesty becomes critical. A final assumption concerns the seller's objective: to transfer the car for a profit. The answer to the original question, then, turns on how to judge the honesty of a stranger, and the relevance of the criteria. In this instance, criteria are often appearance, speech, the presence of value-laden symbols such as fraternal, political, or academic insignia, and any idiosyncrasies that positively or negatively remind the shopper of other people.

What alternative criteria are available to our shopper? Perhaps the reputation of the car lot or showroom, access to other customers of the salesman, consultation with an expert auto mechanic, or a legally watertight warranty. If, however, the shopper chooses to test-drive the car, an opportunity to check out any other criteria depends on the automobile not exploding and killing the driver as soon as the ignition is turned on. Margin for error in decision making is proportional to the magnitude of the outcome. A decision based on taste or preference such as "shall I wear a green sweater with blue slacks?" is unlikely to have irreversible consequences. Decisions based on the *accuracy* of information are of a different order and can be ranked not only according to their immediate consequences but also on how they affect future opportunity to revise the decisions. Because information is a mediated commodity, that is, we are not born "knowing," the process of acquiring, processing, and acting on information becomes increasingly critical as we face decisions leading to increasingly irreversible outcomes.

ACQUIRING INFORMATION

Because my theme is war and peace, not used cars or green sweaters, some time should be spent considering how people acquire information which ultimately leads adults to decisions about issues of war and peace. Very young children delight or drive their parents to despair with questions about why the sky is blue or the stove is hot and how the sun comes up, flowers grow, or babies are born. The first mediators of information are the adults who rear children. Simultaneously, for most of us, television has been an omnipresent mediator. Then comes the authority of educators and their tools: films, textbooks, magazines, newspapers, and the whole range of literature. Think of how often you have said or heard, "My teacher says ... ," "the book, newspaper ... or whatever ... says ... ." Unfortunately, early childhood spontaneous inquiry tends to diminish with increasing exposure to the imbalance in authority between youth and age, or novice and expert, and the unpleasant penalties that often follow on challenging that imbalance. Indeed, in many families, schools, and jobs we receive contradictory messages that abstractly place a high value on thinking independently but concretely punish those whose independent thinking questions the prevailing wisdom of people in power.

The creation of prevailing wisdom is itself timeless and has become a thriving industry for the marketing of people, products, and ideas. A simple example familiar to all Americans is the story of George Washington chopping down a family cherry tree, and later virtuously admitting his act to his father with those legendary words, "I cannot tell a lie." If, as for me, that story registered in your young memory and you rarely thought about it again, its origin may be of interest. I would not have thought about its origin if not for this presentation. The anecdote is one of several apocryphal tales created by Parson Mason Weems, a very early biographer of Washington, who wished to impress contemporary youth with an authoritative model of rectitude (Weems, 1932). This fiction may be the single example of Washington's character remembered by millions of school children. It is a simple example of myth making or marketing.

Textbooks

How about the textbooks that have provided so much basic information about our history? Like the used-car salesman, entrepreneurs who produce textbooks are in business to make a profit. They have to be concerned about how many books they sell because they do not rely on advertising for their revenue. In *America Revised*, Frances FitzGerald (1979) provided an eye-opening study of 19th and 20th century elementary and secondary school textbook production in the United States. She traces a long-standing debate between schools of education and universities concerning the purpose of history as moral example, as citizenship training, or as social science. The book jacket succinctly states "What she finds is that most parties to the debate have one thing in common: their purpose is not so much to inform as to manipulate children."

FitzGerald (1979) characterized contemporary history texts, with rare exception, as "consensus documents" tailored by publishers to accommodate the biases of state and local purchasing committees. The composition and practices of these committees vary so widely in our decentralized education system that publishers retain special employees to keep abreast of local procedures. These committees are, in turn, influenced by citizen pressure groups. States or regions whose purchases amount to millions of dollars have a strong voice in dictating the content and viewpoint of texts, particularly for elementary schools. In our open society there exists no "Department of Censorship," but the need to sell books induces publishers to censor their own texts as circumstances require. The range of this practice boggles the mind. Some national publishers in the mid–1950s, economically burned by right-wing pressure groups, voluntarily submitted textbook manuscripts to an Indiana State Textbook Commission member whose views may be deduced from her stand that books containing the Robin Hood story should be banned because Robin Hood was a Communist, presumably for stealing from the rich to give to the poor (FitzGerald, 1979, p. 38). The Texas Commission required a loyalty oath from textbook writers and a view of history consistent with that standard. Subsequently, an interesting change came about in Texas. In 1985, Governor Mark White abolished the elected state Board of Education because the inferior reputation of Texas public schools hampered his efforts to attract needed new business to replace the declining oil and gas industry. A *New York Times* (1985) article reported that "many political and business leaders felt that the old board had held Texas up to national ridicule by yielding to the pressures of fundamentalists" (pp. 1, 15) in their choice of textbooks. Nonetheless, at a November 1985 meeting to review junior and senior high school texts, the new board appointed by the Governor voted 10 to 0 to require that all history texts print political affiliations, if known, next to the names of any persons quoted in the texts. A front page story in the *Dallas Times Herald* reported that decision, and the reaction of minorities and civil rights activists who asserted that such a requirement was pushing Texas to the brink of McCarthyism and anticommunist hysteria. The following day the board reversed itself to protect Texas from once again being held up to national scorn. The economic imperative of bringing business revenue to the state finally overcame the power of regional prejudice.

Not until the mid–1960s were publishers influenced by progressives and minorities who were inspired by the civil rights movement. This impact began in large northern cities such as Detroit and Newark, New Jersey, whose populations had become predominantly Black following the in-migration of southern Blacks after World War II. Fitz Gerald (1979) reported that a 1964 text called *New York: Past and Present* contained only a passing reference to Blacks. In 1966, the same publisher issued *The New York Story* containing five chapters on Blacks (FitzGerald, 1979). These rapid, expensive revisions proceeded apace with demands from successive groups of excluded or misrepresented minorities. At the conclusion of this chapter, FitzGerald stated,

> Today, texts are written backward or inside out, as it were, beginning with public demand and ending with the historian. This system gives the publishers a certain security, since their books cannot be too far out of the mainstream. But ... they have created another (risk) of a different order. By casting away scholarly claims to authority, they have set themselves adrift on the uncertain seas of public opinion ... . It is difficult when opinions are divided or are changing rapidly, and ... when as happens frequently, people do not really know what they want to hear. (pp. 69–70)

Not until the mid-1970s did the former Confederate States accept changes in the once-racist content that they had required in their textbooks. Today, with the services of computers, publishers can easily keep tabs on current taboos in language, substance, or bias in various regions of the country; can determine the economic consequences associated with the distribution of a general or specialized text; and can then construct a manuscript accordingly.

Even literature has been the target of self-appointed morals and clean-mind-keepers of our society who have clout in proportion to their book-buying budgets. For generations Shakespeare has been rewritten to conform to the requirements of local arbiters of decency. One simple yet graphic example is Dorothy Wickenden's (1985) description of the contemporary laundering of *Romeo and Juliet*: In Act V, Romeo's line, "Well, Juliet, I will *lie* [italics added] with thee tonight" is sanitized to read "Well, Juliet, I will *be* [italics added] with thee tonight."

One positive conclusion can be drawn from this sorry account. The United States is a pluralistic society with an ebb and flow of competing points of view and between bigots of whatever persuasion and the disinformation they impose on children, there is the countervailing force of groups who trust children enough to let them know how history really evolved and what authors of timeless literature really wrote. Wickenden's (1985) concluding sentence is optimistic: "Covert or open, censorship is a doomed enterprise, for it stimulates precisely that dangerous urge it set out to crush: curiosity."

I have taken this much time on textbook manufacture because until recently, the topic has aroused few questions. Yet, reading textbooks may be the most commonly shared experience among us. Because public education provides the most pervasive process for shaping history and social outlook for children, its tools are surely an example of the need for healthy skepticism about the transmission of information, and the power of money in manufacturing that information.

Television

Other media depend primarily on advertising revenue for their profits. The review process leading to self-censorship in these industries may be more fluid because their products are remade daily or weekly, permitting more latitude for variety than the biennial or triennial schedules of textbook publishers. Before the advent of television, A. J. Liebling, a famous analyst of journalism, wrote a regular feature, called *The Wayward Press* for the *New Yorker* magazine. Journalism school students challenged him to support his view that the United States did not have as free a press as was generally assumed. Liebling asked whether they would be surprised to learn that in a private club whose admission criteria required annual incomes of $5 to $10 million, the members held essentially conservative views. The students were not surprised. He then pointed out that newspaper publishers comprise just such a club.

Television has become the single most powerful instrument of mass communication. With its growth and the simultaneous development of sophisticated behavioral science techniques, perception management has reached an all-time peak for assessing and shaping public opinion. The panoply of skills available in Hollywood for the creation of illusion to entertain us, is now applied to designing our reality. Press conferences and newscasts are stage-managed to enhance our confidence in their reliability. Political candidates for the presidency and lesser offices hire specialists to manage their personal marketing, a practice to which the public has so completely adapted that it has given rise to a new highly paid profession. These specialists manage the grooming, speech-training, public-speaking style, and even weight control programs of candidates whose live TV appearances and taped commercials influence many voters more than the substance of the aspirant's platform. This form of packaging is not unlike the construction of textbooks and is adapted for regional consumption much as textbooks are.

Creating Images

A component of image making and myth building that additionally complicates the assessment of information is the perversion of language. What do you think of when you hear "Peacekeeper"? It evokes something benign, even nurturing. That was President Reagan's pet name for the Pershing II cruise missile whose installation in European countries in 1985 triggered outpourings of protest in England, Germany, and elsewhere. Why? Because the Pershing II is, in fact, a deadly nuclear weapon intended for attack, not defense, and designed to reach Soviet cities in approximately 15 min from their European bases.

"Star Wars," the popular name for President Reagan's Strategic Defense Initiative (SDI), has not only generated intense debate in this country and among our Allies but also became the central stumbling block in the Geneva arms control negotiations between the United States and the Soviet Union. The President declared that the SDI is a defensive nonnuclear laser-beam shield that will protect us from enemy nuclear aggression and offered to share it with the Soviets. What does a laser-beam bring to mind? Some wonderful new technique for conducting surgery? *Friends of SDI*—that is their official title, like *Friends of the Earth*—produced a 4-min animated color cartoon as a television commercial. The visual is a child's drawing of a house and a smiling sun in the sky, flowers and, if I recall accurately, pets romping around the yard. The audio is a child's lovely sing-song voice saying, "My Daddy told me that the SDI is the President's way of keeping everybody safe. | A kind of plexiglass dome appears over the drawing, and little red missiles bounce off it.| My Daddy says that the SDI means that nobody can win wars anymore, so why would anybody start one? My Daddy is smart." The plexiglass is then joined by a rainbow. The only thing her smart Daddy and the President did not say is "Instead of building SDIs, get rid of the missiles."

At the drawing-board stage of SDI, there is general agreement among our own scientists that total population protection is infeasible. It was disputed, however, that the laser could be activated without nuclear power, a possibility dismissed by the scientists in this country who opposed it, and apparently by Soviet scientists. As conceived, the SDI would have required thousands of these nuclear weapons in constant orbit, passing over the Soviet Union twice a day, with no watertight warranty against accidental or intentional detonation. It is not surprising that the Soviets viewed SDI as a first strike weapon and an aggressive escalation of the arms race.

In 1986, it was clear that the cost of SDI research would entail tens of billions of dollars annually into the unforeseeable future, added to an armaments budget that had already dismantled or subordinated domestic programs to low priority status. Funds for urban housing, food stamps, student loans, road and bridge repair, public transportation, *ad infinitum*, were cut to reduce a staggering federal deficit already attributable to arms manufacture and the maintenance of a defense establishment. Justification for this lopsided use of taxpayers' dollars was the threat of an implacable enemy, an evil empire, the inhuman, aggressive Soviet Union.

Consider the following statement of a U.S. President:

> We concur in considering [their] government … as totally without morality, insolent
> beyond bearing, inflated with vanity and ambition, aiming at the exclusive domination
> of the sea, lost in corruption, of deep-rooted hatred towards us, hostile to liberty wher-
> ever it endeavors to show its head, and the eternal disturber of the peace of the world.

The President was Thomas Jefferson (1904), in his June 12, 1815 letter to
Thomas Leiper, describing England. If we review our own history, or that of any
other country, the candidates for the role of evil empire have shifted steadily over
relatively short intervals. Japan and Germany, our enemies during World War II,
enjoy more felicitous relations with us today than Russia or, even, France—our
Allies during that same war, and Thomas Jefferson's eternal disturber of the peace,
England, is today our closest friend.

THE DANGER IN MARKETING WEAPONS

The marketing of enemies is not too different from the marketing of textbooks or the
selling of candidates. The process invites people to surrender thinking for themselves because some authority defines the facts for them. In respect to weapons, lay-
men are offered soothing assurances, and again cajoled to surrender independent
judgment because the science of weaponry is so complex. It is essential that we de-
mystify nuclear weapons that have little to do with security and everything to do with
an astronomically profitable industry for the few paid for by the many. The arsenals
of the major nuclear powers have had the capacity to blow up the world since before
some of us were born. The arms race threatens rather than buttresses our security and
adulterates the quality of life for vast segments of our population.

The "Perfect" Torpedoes

Bear with me as I describe to you a little-known aspect about our weapons during
World War II, our submarine torpedoes that were *perfect* on the drawing board.
This account is provided by Edward L. Beach (1980) who served as commander of
three submarines during World War II. His article appeared in *The American Heritage* and is based, as Beach stated at the outset, on surreptitiously retained files of
war-patrol reports.

In October 1942, while submerged in Pacific waters, Beach's crew fired a vol-
ley of torpedoes at an unescorted enemy tanker. Hearing an explosion in the distance they were certain that they had hit their target. Soon after, a violent explosion
close by shook their own submarine with considerable force, causing Beach to
think they were hit, but he was wrong.

Later that night, Beach, himself, aimed four torpedoes at another target. The first two hit the target. The third jogged to the left, ran a quarter circle, straightened out, but missed the target. The fourth went straight for the center of the target, passed under it and kept going, "visible in the distance for two miles beyond the stricken ship" (1980, p. 42).

Afterwards the crew held a post-mortem to figure out what could be wrong with their torpedoes. They finally concluded that the first two hits on their target, heard and timed correctly, had probably failed to damage it, just as the violent explosion had shaken, but not damaged their own submarine. Beach came to a further disturbing conclusion. The cause of the explosion near his own sub was one of his own torpedoes that had circled back to its starting point. He realized that their target had escaped because the torpedoes had run in a circle, and run deep, and had faulty magnetic sensors, and through a fourth unrelated defect, they frequently exploded just before reaching their targets. So, as a result of one defect, his own torpedo almost blew up his own ship, and as a result of another defect, it exploded above the submarine, saving their lives.

He struggled to explain this debacle, given that the United States had an excellent submarine force, fine ships, and well-trained and highly motivated crews. He became aware as time went on that our subs could protect themselves in enemy waters but they could scarcely hurt the enemy at all.

Beach concluded:

> Most inexcusable, those in ultimate authority refused to accept the continually renewed evidence that there was something wrong. All unsuccessful attacks, without exception, were blamed on the skippers, their fire-control parties and their torpedo-overhaul personnel. We knew both British and German submarines had had similar problems which were solved by a few weeks of driven work (Admiral Doenitz is said to have refused to send any more U-boats on patrol until their torpedoes were fixed). Yet impassioned demands for similar investigation of ours were put aside. Our technical experts had produced a perfect weapon, which by the mechanical marvel of its design, could only function correctly and could never fail to function correctly .... Any other explanations were merely self-serving excuses (of the skippers).
>
> In brief, while German, British, Italian and Japanese torpedoes functioned well, ours performed so poorly that had they been the subject of deliberate sabotage they hardly could have been worse ...
>
> Our submarines were commanded by men who were products of a system that penalized those who questioned too hard the established order of things. None were rebels, none were warriors, although some ... clearly possessed the requisite potential .... They were, in short, what they had been trained to be. (1980, p. 42–43)

Although there is much more, I will cite only one last sentence from Beach:

> Nothing can be more demoralizing to men who must risk their lives in combat than to be forced to use weapons which, they know from experience, are not dependable, and

for which they have no substitute … unless it be stubborn, unrealistic opposition by "experts" who, in the face of evidence refuse even to investigate it. (1980, p. 46)

No great leap of the imagination is required to contemplate an intercontinental ballistic missile, which can be described as an airborne torpedo, circling on itself and returning to Kansas or some other home base.

CONCLUSION

The critical moral of this long story: Exercise your greatest skepticism toward men in power who are more enamored of a weapon than of negotiation. Exercise your greatest skepticism toward these men when they market pet weapons on the strength of expert opinion that they have purchased because it conforms to their own fantasies.

There are lesser risks for exercising skepticism than those recorded by Beach. You can be called negative, cynical, paranoid, or even, unpatriotic. These are not pleasant labels. As for the payoffs, each person, individually, has to assess these. In today's nuclear environment an irreversible error cannot be written off by saying "Oops!" Drawing-board perfect devices may not be testable except in the actual conditions for which they were designed. I am not advocating that we should be seeking better weapons; rather, distrust of weapons designers and salesmen.

If you ask, "What difference does my skepticism make?" I will reply "If your skepticism doesn't have merit and doesn't have power, why are so many experts and authorities telling you to leave the thinking to them?"

BIOGRAPHICAL NOTE

In 1998, Doris Miller retired from private practice in New York City. She moved to Haverford, PA, where, with like-minded senior citizens, she is active in antiwar and antinuclear weapons programs and patriotic protection of our civil rights. Her Ph.D. is from New York University.

REFERENCES

Beach, E. L. (1980). Culpable negligence: A submarine commander tells why we almost lost the Pacific war. *The American Heritage, 32*(1), 41–54.

FitzGerald, F. (1979) *America revised.* Boston: Atlantic Monthly Press.

Jefferson, T. (1904). *The works of Thomas Jefferson (The Federal Edition). Volume XI: Correspondance and papers 1815.* New York: G. P. Putnam's Sons.

New York Times. (1985, December 3). Section C, pp. 1, 15.

Weems, M. L.(1932). *An anecdote form the life of George Washington, from the history of a very extraordinary man written by the Rev. M. L. Weems.* Madison, NJ: The Golden Hind Press.

Wickenden, D. (1985, May 25). Bowdlerizing the Bard. *The Baltimore Sun.*

PEACE AND CONFLICT: JOURNAL OF PEACE PSYCHOLOGY, 11(4), 419–425

REVIEWS

Hope in a Dark Time: Reflections on Humanity's Future, David Krieger (Ed.), 2004. Santa Barbara, CA: Capra Press.

Is There Really Hope for Peace?

Marc Pilisuk

Saybrook Graduate School and the University of California

As the director of The Nuclear Age Peace Foundation, Dave Kreiger has, as much as anyone, studied the grim possibilities that face us if we do not find a way to peace. In dark times we are prone to pin our hopes on the success of little projects that bring peace or viability to some small place in the world. However, Krieger is a realist who understands well the magnitude of the global threat. The danger regards not only a host of separate problems calling for creative solutions but a recognition that these are parts of a larger system moving toward its own demise. I approached his anthology, *Hope in a Dark Time: Reflections on Humanity's Future*, wishing for a new insight to justify optimism, but fearing that I would find only a description of inspiring but small projects that never seem sufficient to turn the corner toward a world of peace. What I gleaned, however, was the possibility that an amalgam of changes, large and small, may well be adding up to something new and hopeful. In these troubled times, that light is something to be cherished.

To appreciate the grounds for hope fully it is essential to review the reasons for despair. The current stage of the industrial development has produced a highly potent set of megacorporations designed to require expansion to be viable. With little accountability for the well-being of communities they touch, they are able to extract the promise of low taxes, the best land, the cheapest labor, the fewest environmental restraints. They provide jobs, in the short term, and then move on to sites that offer more profitable options. They are cutting the rainforests, usurping the

Correspondence should be addressed to Marc Pilisuk, 494 Cragmont Ave., Berkeley, CA 94708. E-mail: mpilisuk@saybrook.edu sources of oil and gas, of arable land and clean water, and undoing the commons that have been developed to provide safety, security, and joy for all humans. Governments have assumed the role of contracting agencies by which education, health, and medical care; national defense; and environmental protection are regarded as commodities that are traded to increase the wealth of a decreasing number of players. Poor nations are obliged to subsidize their own destitution through the interest they must pay on their development loans to wealthy centers of finance (Perkins, 2004). In another anthology, The International Forum on Globalization presents a rich understanding of corporate globalization and of the alternatives needed to change it (Cavanagh & Mander, 2004).

Many are already victims of this global change. Wars of the past half century inflicting disproportionate civilian casualties have, in large measure, reflected the quest for control over resources (Klare, 2002; Wolf, 1999). Known carcinogens are unregulated, schools lack funds, and low wage jobs do not support a family. The global market makes weapons readily available, and violence is repeatedly presented as normal without need for examination of its roots (Pilisuk, 1998, 2001; Winter, Pilisuk, Houck, & Lee, 2001). Many people have been reduced to competing for places in a refugee camp or a homeless shelter or for jobs in sweatshops. Many poor communities are vying for the repositories of toxic wastes. Some of the displaced are forced into the vast trafficking of young women or of illegal drugs or into the epidemic of forced child labor. Some of the displaced have become angry at the U.S. government but also at their own pro-corporate governments that remain in power by military support, without which they would be unable to stem the rising dissent. Some of the displaced have opposed what they perceive as arrogance of a government that disregards international law while insisting that its model of enterprise and of government is universal. Among the opponents are labor, community, and religious leaders who are being harassed or killed by paramilitary groups. Some as individuals, others as parts of larger networks, have determined to strike back violently and have provided the current rationale for a continuing state of warfare, sustained by fear, against ill-defined terrorism. Its daily toll is high but is minimized by an increasingly centralized corporate media that reinforces the message of what is most important: shopping, promotion of the self, the lives of entertainment celebrities, and the punishment of those who act out against "decent" people (McChesney, 1997). Even the public language of values and morality has been shaped to justify arrogance, greed, restrictions on human rights, and torture (Lakoff, 1996).

The military response to opponents of U.S. corporate and military hegemony is particularly worrisome in the arena of nuclear weapons. Recent military collaboration between major powers China and Russia, the militarization of outer space, the proliferation of nuclear weapon states, the rollback of treaty obligations that held some prospects for diminishing the risks of nuclear war are matters that merit concern, the more so for the low level of public attention directed to these dangers. Are the human capacities for psychic numbing (Lifton, 1995), for denial, and for distraction (Milburn & Conrad, 1996) an inevitable ally of those who promote force in the pursuit of growth, wealth, and power? Collective denial is part of the problem. One is reminded of studies by Hannah Arendt (2004) showing how unbelieving the German people were of the magnitude of what was happening during the rise of Hitler. Would we know if we had gradually entered the worlds of perpetual degradation foreseen by Aldous Huxley and George Orwell many years ago? It is with awareness of the danger that we grasp for signs of change.

The search for hope in this book begins with a foreword by Desmond Tutu reminding us that one does not rely on external light to show the path through a dark tunnel, but on an inner light that strengthens our resolve. With it, and in a remarkable process of nonviolent forgiveness and reconciliation, Nelson Mandela emerged from 27 years in prison to lead the country that had tried to silence him. Tutu explains that the African word, *ubuntu*, means we can only be human together. Krieger's introduction argues that hope is not always rational within the perimeters of what is known. Hope must sometimes be irrational and dependent on events we cannot quite foresee. Surely that was the case for the hope that led to the actions by Gandhi and Martin Luther King. The question then changes from whether we are correct in having hope, to whether we, by our actions, can create the hope that will make the world a better place. We do this without a map to highlight just what actions will be amplified beyond our power to foresee the future. Bill Cane's chapter noted that Lincoln's assassination depressed his friend D. D. Addams, whose daughter, Jane Addams was then motivated to establish the settlement houses giving hope to a generation of immigrants. Jane Addams's Hull house was visited by Myles Horton who returned to Tennessee inspired to create the Highlander School to promote racial integration and social change. Martin Luther King recommended Rosa Parks for a stay at the school, just weeks before she refused to move to the back of the bus. However, what actions are right for the rest of us? Whatever they are, Cane reminded us that good actions, however small, need endless repetition and that there is great power in personal communication.

Joanna Macy's contribution is to describe a revolutionary turn that is already well underway. It is not being televised, and it may or may not succeed. Yet it is plainly visible. The great turning has three elements. The first is activism, which includes the organized efforts to curtail the abuses of the environment and to oppose the rush to war and the mistreatment of people. The second is the support of system change by starting to play under different rules, for example, creating alternative indexes to the Gross National Product that include quality of life and health for all people, beginning new methods of land holding, cohousing, fair trade practices to prevent exploited labor, use of renewables, and local and sustainable food practices. The third is a revolution in consciousness, a scientific and spiritual convergence emphasizing connections and interdependence rather than boundaries and competitive acquisition. The book does not deal with George Lakoff's (1996) work suggesting that some changes in consciousness have been in the opposite direction. Lakoff has argued that an extreme conservative position, focusing on highly disciplined pursuit of self-centered interests, is being favored among those who have been raised with punitive models of the family. This latter model of thought, so diametrically opposed to a worldview emphasizing interdependence and caring, appears to me, however, to reflect a limited view of psychological development. Even those reared in authoritarian, father-dominated households may have potentials for a universal caring outlook. In fact, the popularity of those self centered and punitive beliefs has required a deliberate and well-funded movement to gain support (Frank, 2004), whereas humanistically oriented change seems to be growing organically. Perhaps one marker of this radical turn toward interdependence and collective well-being can be seen in Frederick Frank's chapter presenting the value of "reverence for life" as the alternative to be embraced if there is to be a future. This value has motivated many of the great humanitarians and now inspires others. We witness a myriad of groups large and small springing up to offer solace, to reflect on where we are, and to provide imaginative new projects.

Krieger's chapter suggests that people are powerful and more compassionate than one would suppose. He cites examples of people who have turned their pain into remarkable examples of healing: the *hibakusha*, atomic bomb survivors who do not let their radiation-induced illness prevent them from traveling the world over to remind people of the horror of nuclear weapons and the need for peace; Hafsat Abiola, a young Nigerian woman (also represented in this collection) whose parents were assassinated for promoting democracy and went on to found the Kundirat Initiative—working for democracy and for women's rights in Africa; the murder of a 12-year-old Pakistani boy who had previously escaped to tell the world of enslaved child laborers led another 12-year-old to create the *Kids Can Save the Children* organization. It is responsible for the liberation of thousands of indentured children. The creator of this new organization, Craig Kiellburger, now in his 20s, contributes a chapter in this volume providing testimony to the unsung powers of children. The group he started is now working in 35 countries, teaching skills of survival, of conflict resolution, and of the dangers of nuclear war. It is responsible for the liberation of thousands of indentured children.

The power of the forgiveness process has barely been tapped. It offers a pride and nobility to those who confess to their part in oppressive actions and seek forgiveness and restoration. This enables once competing parts of the human community to live peacefully without fear of retribution. Barbara Marx Hubbard adds the power of evolutionary consciousness. The same power that melded subatomic particles into living forms in viable settings is still alive in the life forms that have evolved. It is visible in the ability of humans to shape the evolutionary process in ways yet beyond our imagination. Daiseku Ikeda shows how a Buddhist view helps us add the hidden powers of connection and empathic dialogue to the tools that bring forth extraordinary accomplishments from ordinary people. Joseph Rotblatt shares the experience of mobilizing scientists to use their knowledge for peace and human betterment. Students pledging to do the same with their future work surely have followed this lead.

Other contributors remind us of the web of international organizations and non-governmental organizations (NGOs) that continues both to alleviate suffering and to promote education, sustainability, and peace. Their work continues in times of special crisis and beyond crises to eradicate the dark time that has befallen us. Elise Boulding notes that, unbeknownst to most of us, the United Nations (UN) quarterly Chronicle reports on its six major bodies, 13 associated bodies, 16 specialized agencies, five regional commissions, 20 research institutes, two Universities, and varying numbers of peacekeeping and observer commissions. Few activist groups assisting refugees are aware of the magnitude of the work of the UN Commission on Refugees, few peace activists are aware of the UN Institute of Disarmament, and few who fight poverty know of the UN Research Institute on Social Development. Boulding sees on the horizon a new model of citizenship, one that shows love for one's community but also for the diversity within one's nation state. Beyond that she sees us as needing to know and love our UN, slow and imperfect bureaucracy that it may be, as the embodiment of our most sacred principles and our commitment to global justice. We also find a large number of NGOs that, like the UN, are working diligently to preserve land, protect environments, feed people and heal them, teach reading and sustainable farming, protect human rights, and insist on visibility and accountability from corporate excess. Psychology has been clearly represented in efforts to build cultures of peace (Wessells, Schwebel, & Anderson, 2001). These groups do not go away when their efforts are sadly not rewarded. Rather they find meaning and satisfaction for their participants, rewards that many are seeking.

One may ask whether the institutional forms needed to sustain and to enhance such activities can possibly evolve with the reach called for in these troubled times. Through formal actions of nation states, efforts to bridge national sovereignty have created the UN and the International Criminal Court. Meanwhile, from the grassroots, unofficial organizations like Witness for Peace and The Non-violent Police Force have appeared on the scene to prevent military violence. Amazingly the world has seen previously unimaginable indigenous participation in the Earth Summit in Rio de Janeiro, the World Conference on Women in Beijing, and the World Social Forum in Porto Allegre. An informal communication network assures that no matter where in the world the small elite of powerful bankers and government officials hold their G7, World Trade Organization, or International Monetary Fund meetings, they will be met by truly massive protests from those whose voices are excluded. A network of e-mail messages contributed to the largest ever global mobilization of people opposing the invasion of Iraq. As that war fails quite visibly, the movement may gain strength in the minds of even greater numbers of people. Falk and Strauss suggest that the forms, already evolving, may soon take a step toward global democracy in the formation of a Global People's Assembly. Such active participation in civil society, though currently frowned on by the governments of China, Russia, and the United States, might nonetheless emerge from a conference of NGOs providing the UN with a model for ratification and support by member states. It might evolve informally by seeking voluntary contributions to provide a continuing platform for peace and social justice activities between annual meetings of the World Social forum.

Several chapters remind us that an individual can publicly declare nonsupport for nuclear weapons or be a teacher of nonviolent practice and that such activities are effective in cementing our connections with larger social forces. Such actions are effective also in the creation of symbols with power to capture the imagination of others. The book includes moving documents. The UN preamble notes that we the people have joined to save succeeding generations from the scourge of war, to reaffirm faith in fundamental human rights, to establish conditions for justice and international law, and to promote social progress. The Earth Charter reminds us of the psychological attributes of creativity, conscience, reflection, language, empathy, and love that make possible the choice of peace. The Universal Declaration of Human Rights establishes a set of conditions that could assure the humanity of the entire human family. Scattered throughout the book are poems of peace and of dedication helping to convey the message that hope is less an assessment of the current state of the world than a matter of our motivation to create a better one.

Is there reason for hope? I look at the ways that corporate globalization and militarism have strengthened their controls over almost everything else. Then I look at the great examples in this book of institutions that have evolved with peace as their mission and of actions of dedicated people that hold unforeseeable power for good. The examples often seem small in relation to the degree of entrenched power that perpetuates endless war to further insatiable greed. Perhaps that is the message—that is, that acts both small and large are occurring even while the old empire hangs on. If we can see them as a tapestry that so many of us are weaving together, then perhaps hope can be justified. As long as people are weaving the strands of peace, justice, sustainability, and reverence for life, then hope will continue beyond any particular war or any particularly disparaging political event. In the poem by the title of its most powerful line, the Dalai Lama tells us what is most vital to the dream, "Never give up." This book is a contribution to that goal and a gift that can provide glimmers of hope, even for realists.

BIOGRAPHICAL NOTE

Marc Pilisuk is a Professor at the Saybrook Graduate School and Research Center in San Francisco and Professor Emeritus at the University of California. He is a past president of the Society for the Study of Peace, Conflict, and Violence and a member of the Steering Committee of the Psychologists for Social Responsibility.

His recent publications deal with globalization, terrorism, citizen participation, and the structure of violence.

REFERENCES

Arendt, H. (2004). *The origins of totalitarianism*. New York: Schoken Books.

Cavanagh, J., & Mander, J. (Eds.). (2004). *Alternatives to economic globalization: A better world is possible.* San Francisco, CA: Barrett-Koehler.

Frank, T. (2004). *What's the matter with Kansas: How conservatives won the heart of America.* New York: Metropolitan Press.

Klare, M. T. (2002). *Resource wars: The new landscape of global conflict.* New York: Henry Holt.

Lakoff, G. (1996). *What conservatives know that liberals don't.* Chicago: University Of Chicago Press.

Lifton, R. J. (with Mitchell, G). (1995). *Hiroshima in America: Fifty years of denial.* New York: Putnam and Avon Books.

McChesney, R. W. (1997). *Corporate media and the threat to democracy.* New York: Seven Stories Press.

Milburn, M. A., & Conrad, S. D. (1996). *The politics of denial.* Cambridge, MA: The MIT Press.

Perkins, J. (2004). *Confessions of an economic hit man.* San Francisco, CA: Barrett-Koehler.

Pilisuk, M. (1998). The hidden structure of contemporary violence. *Peace and Conflict: Journal of Peace Psychology, 4,* 197–216.

Pilisuk, M. (2001). Humanistic psychology and peace. In K. Schneider, J. Bugental, & F. Pierson (Eds.). *Handbook of humanistic psychology* (pp. 115–126). Thousand Oaks, CA: Sage.

Wessells, M., Schwebel, M., & Anderson, A. (2001). Psychologists making a difference in the public arena: Building cultures of peace. In D. J. Christie, R.V. Wagner, and D. D. Winter, (Eds.). *Peace, conflict, and violence: Peace psychology for the 21st century* (pp. 350–362). Englewood, NJ: Prentice Hall.

Winter, D., Pilisuk, M., Houck, S. & Lee. M. (2001). Maintaining militarism: Money, masculinity, and the search for the mystical. In D. J. Christie, R. V. Wagner, & D. C. Winter, (Eds.) *Peace, conflict, and violence: Peace psychology for the 21st Century* (pp. 139–148). Englewood, NJ: Prentice Hall.

Wolf, E. (1999). *Peasant wars of the twentieth century.* Norman: University of Oklahoma Press.

PEACE AND CONFLICT: JOURNAL OF PEACE PSYCHOLOGY, *11*(4), 426
Copyright © 2005, Lawrence Erlbaum Associates, Inc.

ACKNOWLEDGEMENTS

I am pleased to acknowledge the invaluable assistance and counsel provided by my three loyal Associate Editors—Tina Montiel, Susan Opotow, and Mike Wessells—the Journal Advisory Board, and the Editorial Board of *Peace and Conflict: Journal of Peace Psychology*. Review Editor Herb Blumberg continues to procure excellent reviews for his section of the journal.

I especially appreciate the expertise and wise counsel of our Assistant to the Editor, Nancy MacLean, as well as the excellent support of Clementine Brasier throughout my tenure as Editor.

Thanks to Amy Bradfield Douglass for serving as resident Statistical Consultant, with the timely assistance of her colleague, Todd Kahan. Thanks also to the Bates College Ladd Library Reference Department, especially Chris Schiff and Laura Juraska. We are indebted as well to Dr. Jose Quiroga for his thoughtful commentary on a manuscript.

I am particularly grateful to Klaus Boehnke, who organized an impressive theme issue on German Peace Psychology, and to Jean Maria Arrigo, who found, encouraged, and aided the efforts of Lt. Col. Dwight Roblyer and Major Walt Schrepel (U.S. Army, ret'd), resulting in one of the most stimulating theme issues of my five editorial years: "Military Ethics and Peace Psychology: A Dialogue." Thanks for educating us.

I am deeply indebted to Bates College, especially to Dean of the Faculty, Jill Reich, for the encouragement and material support I have received. My task as Editor would be infinitely more difficult without it.

Finally: Jaclyn—thanks for your production skill and persistence and good humor—and insistence that we meet our deadlines, which we've finally done.

Richard V. Wagner
Editor

PEACE AND CONFLICT: JOURNAL OF PEACE PSYCHOLOGY, 11(4), 427–428
Copyright © 2005, Lawrence Erlbaum Associates, Inc.

INDEX TO VOLUME 11, 2005

ARTICLES

Anderson, A. *Doris K. Miller and Psychologists for Social Responsibility.* 393

Arrigo, J. *Introduction to a Dialogue Between Peace Psychology and Military Ethics.* 1

Boehnke, K. *Once a Peacenik—Always a Peacenik? Results from a German Six-Wave, Nineteen-Year Longitudinal Study.* 337

Boehnke, K. *Peace Psychology in Germany.* 229

Boehnke, M. (see Boehnke, K.)

Boos, M. (see Kolbe, M.)

Brähler, E. (see Stellmacher, J.)

Cairns, E. (see Moeschberger, S.)

Cohrs, J. *Personal Values and Attitudes Toward War.* 293

Darley, J.(see Wolfe, R.)

Deutsch, M. *Commentary on Morality, Decision Making, and Collateral Casualties.* 63

Dixon, D. (see Moeschberger, S.)

Eidelson, R. *Self and Nation: A Comparison of Americans' Beliefs Before and After 9/11.* 153

Frindte, W. *Old and New Anti-Semitic Attitudes in the Context of Authoritarianism and Social Dominance Orientations—Two Studies in Germany.* 239

Fuss, D. (see Boehnke, K.)

Gurtner, A. (see Kolbe, M.)

Heider, F. *Violence and Ecology.* 9

Hogenraad, R. *What the Words of War Can Tell Us About the Risk of War.* 137

Kelman, H. *The Psychological Impact of the Sadat Visit on Israeli Society.* 111

Kielmann, S. (see Cohrs, J.)

Kindervater, A. (see Boehnke, K.)

Kolbe, M. *Social Identity in Times of International Conflict.* 313

Koop, I. *Refugees in Church Asylum: Psychological Peace Intervention between Political Conflicts and Individual Suffering.* 355

Levinger, G. *Five Obstacles Facing Military Ethics: Comment on "Beyond Precision."* 41

Maes, J. (see Cohrs, J.)

McKay, S. *Pioneers in Peace Psychology: Doris Miller.* 369

Miller, D. *The Risks and Payoffs of Skepticism.* 409

Moeschberger, S. *Forgiveness in Northern Ireland: A Model for Peace in the Midst of the "Troubles."* 199

Moschner, B. (see Cohrs, J.)

Myers-Bowman, K. *"Differences Between War and Peace are Big:" Children from Yugoslavia and the United States Describe Peace and War.* 177

Myers-Walls, J. (See Myers-Bowman, K.)

Niens, U. (see Moeschberger, S.)

Pepitone, A. *Comments on Paras and Centurions."* 91

Pilisuk, M. *Unprofessional Warriors: Lesson Small and Large.* 95

Plummer, M. (see Eidelson, R.)

Roblyer, D. *Beyond Precision: Morality, Decision Making, and Collateral Casualties.* 17

Roblyer, D. *Response to Four Commentaries on "Beyond Precision."* 67

Roe, M. (see McKay, S.)

Rust. J. (see Heider. F.)

Schrepel. W. *Paras and Centurions: Lessons Learned From the Battle of Algiers.* 71

Schrepel. W. *Responding to Comments on "Paras and Centurions."* 105

Schwebel. M. *Can Wars Be Just?* 47

Schwebel. M. *Peace Activism and Courage.* 397

Sommer. G. (see Stellmacher. J.)

Stellmacher. J. *The Cognitive Representation of Human Rights: Knowledge, Importance and Commitment.* 267

Tobach. E. *Being a Pioneer: How Many Ways and How Many Days?* 387

Wagner. R. V. *A Welcome Exposure to Peace Psychology in Germany.* 227

Wagner. R. V. *The Activist Psychologist: Doris K. Miller.* 367

Wagner. R. V. (see Arrigo. J.)

Walker. K. (see Myers-Bowman. K.)

Wammetsberger. D. (see Frindte. W.)

Weiner. M. (see Heider. F.)

Wessells. M. (see McKay. S.)

Wettig. S. (see Frindte. W.)

Winter. A. *Battle of Algiers/Battle of Baghdad.* 101

Wolfe. R. *Protracted Asymmetrical Conflict Erodes Standards for Avoiding Civilian Casualties.* 55

Zahm. B. *My Colleague and Friend. Doris Miller.* 391

REVIEWS

Chan. C. *Demanding Higher Standards: Evaluating the Effectiveness of International Interventions.* 215

Goldstein. J. *Perspective on Violence.* 219

Hutchings. K. *Making Conflict Constructive.* 223

Pilisuk. M. *Is There Really Hope for Peace?* 419